I0027213

CIRCUS

The Amazing story of the circus stars and legends that have entertained America for over 200 years.

TERRY W. LYONS

Circus by Terry W. Lyons
Copyright © 2016
ISBN 978-0-9971530-7-1
Library of Congress Control Number: 2016919186
Cover Image: Shutterstock

All rights reserved. No part of this book may be reproduced, stored in a retrieval system, or transmitted in any form or by any means without the prior written permission of the publishers, except by a reviewer who may quote brief passages in a review printed in a newspaper, magazine, or journal.

LA
Maison

La Maison Publishing, Inc.
Vero Beach Florida
The Hibiscus City
lamaisonpublishing@gmail.com

Acknowledgments

Without the help of generous friends, writing this book would simply not have been possible. It is not only the advice and suggestions that friends offer, it is the encouragement that is so important.

First, my father who took me to "The Greatest Show on Earth" and awakened my interest and love for the circus. Writing this book certainly brought back memories of a wonderful time in my life.

Without the patience, and typing ability of my wife, Babs, the book would not have made it to publication. No one else could read my writing.

Once again, Neil Stalter provided the judgement and editorial review to make CIRCUS possible. Neil's suggestions and guidance were not only helpful, but always encouraging. Neil was also a key ingredient in reviewing and offering advice for each of my first two books, "Bar Hopping Thru America" and *"Drinking Around The World."*

My original mentor, Gene Hull, author of several wonderful books, provided valuable suggestions along the way. Gene's most recent book, "Slice Of Life" is a joy to read.

Don Casey reviewed the beginning drafts and encouraged me to keep going and complete the book. Then, although battling cancer, Don managed to read the book in one day and offered many thoughtful suggestions.

John Burke, who knows a lot about the circus, offered valuable advice and helped keep the many dates and facts correct.

Our son, David, was a source of needed assistance whenever the computer became a major obstacle, which seemed to be way too often.

And Janet Sierzant, La Maison Publisher, certainly went "the extra mile" in accommodating my many requests. Janet is also an author of several books including "Gemini Joe."

The Howard Brothers Model Circus is part of the Ringling Brothers Circus Museum located in Sarasota, Florida. Built by one man, Howard Tibbals, this replica of Ringling Brothers Circus is the largest miniature circus in the world. It has 1300 miniature circus personnel, 900 animals, 150 circus wagons and is displayed in a special 10,000 square foot building.

INTRODUCTION

The bright, colorful posters, the clowns, the gaily-decorated wagons, the exotic animals and the acrobats performing incredible feats-- I have always loved the circus. It generates such excitement of the pure, wonderful, and innocent variety. The tents, the announcers and the stirring music, simply add to the fun.

I had forgotten about the circus. That happens as you grow older and excitement isn't the type of entertainment at the top of your list. You are more interested in a cruise, a guided tour, a dinner at a fancy restaurant, a wonderful golf course, or a game of bridge...things that include the word "easy" in their description. My hometown, Olean, N. Y., has a tradition of holding a high school reunion every year and all classes are invited, so it's a pretty big deal with over a thousand people attending each year. Attending a recent reunion with my wife, a fellow graduate, I met an old friend who lived a few houses away when we were growing up. We chatted about many things as you do when you encounter a friend after over 20 years. At one point in the conversation, Jim said "Terry, whatever happened to that miniature circus you built one summer. You had tents and wagons----even miniature people? All the wagons were painted bright red and "LYONS CIRCUS" was stenciled in white on the side of each one." Well, I have no idea whatever happened to my circus; but I was reminded that Sarasota, Florida was the home of the Ringling Brothers Circus Museum and a miniature circus was part of the attraction. When we returned to our hometown, Vero Beach, Florida, I decided to pay a visit to the museum. Without any doubt, The Howard Brothers Model Circus, built by one man, is absolutely as amazing as any of the circus performances described in this book.

Viewing the miniature circus and other exhibits at the museum revived all the wonderful memories of "the circus coming to town," the bright posters, colorful trains, enormous tents, lions and tigers, acrobats, clowns, and the "man on the flying trapeze." So I decided to write a book about a period in American history that was simply "wonderful."

The circus can be traced back to the Romans and events in the Coliseum; but the first "modern circus" was staged in London in 1768 and the circus appeared in America a few years later. The "golden years" of the circus in this country included the first half of the 20th century. Over 100 circuses were crisscrossing America in 1900 and by 1920 over 20 circuses were travelling by railroad. Some of these early shows were big, such as Hagenbeck and Wallace, Barnum and Bailey, Sells Floto and Ringling Brothers, and they were competitive. The 1920's witnessed a consolidation in the business and the winner was Ringling Brothers who had purchased Barnum and Bailey in 1906. In 1919, Ringling's decided to combine the two shows and call it "The Greatest Show on Earth," and at the time, this was probably a true statement. Travelling on four trains, with over 1,500 employees and hundreds of animals, using a tent that occupied over two acres and accommodated 12,000 people, the circus was a "big deal" when it arrived in over 100 towns across America. In fact, it was such a big deal that many smaller towns declared the arrival "Circus Day" and most of the town, businesses, schools, and even factories, closed for the day. Special excursion trains brought people to town from distant villages in the county.

My father was a big fan of the circus and this book is based on my dad and I attending a performance of Ringling Brothers in Olean, New York, when I was a young boy. The show under the Big Top with three rings and four stages included 23 featured acts (called displays in the circus), and as each major performance takes place, I capture here the significance of the act by describing the lives of the most famous and talented acrobats, aerialists, daredevils, clowns, freaks, and many of the animals who became celebrities.

In addition to a description of the stars of the past hundred years, this book explains the incredible mechanics of the travelling circus town: the Pullman and animal cars on the trains, the dining tent that served 5,000 meals to over 1500 people every day, the "set-up" and the "tear down" of over 40 tents each day. It also covers the care, training, and transportation of hundreds of wild animals and the talented performers and producers who brought this spectacle to life for thousands of Americans every summer.

Envision yourself under a huge canvas attempting to watch three rings, four stages, high in the air or in cages on the ground—all at once with band music blaring, people laughing and cheering, the odor of popcorn, hay, sawdust, lemonade, hot dogs, the circus transported you to a dream for two hours. This book offers "children of all ages" a ringside seat to the circus and its stars, one of the oldest and greatest entertainment vehicles of all time. "Enjoy the show!"

Posters announcing, "the circus is coming to town" appeared about a month before the designated arrival date. They appeared tacked to telephone poles, in store windows, on huge billboards, and covered the entire side of barns out in the country.

CIRCUS

TERRY W. LYONS

The gravesite of Lillian Leitzel and the love of her life, Alfredo Codona, in Inglewood, California, depicts the two circus stars in a flying embrace, like angels.

Table of Contents

Terry W. Lyons

THE ARRIVAL

My first indication that the circus was coming to town occurred one May morning on my walk from home to Grade School Number Two in Olean, N.Y. In the 1930's, 40's, and 50's when I was growing up, Olean was a city in Western New York State with a population of about 21,000 and an oil refinery smack in the center of town.

There were seven grade schools and one high school and everyone walked to and from school, including coming home for an hour for lunch. The lunch hour passed quickly since we had to walk the round trip of about a quarter mile each way, eat lunch, and squeeze in a snowball fight in the winter and games of marbles, "catch" and basketball in the spring and fall.

Not a lot of big things happened in a town the size of Olean, and, of course, there was no television or computer social network; in fact, in the 30's and 40's the telephone was just beginning to catch on. So, seeing that colorful poster with a lion practically jumping off the page tacked to a telephone pole at the corner of 12th and State Street was big news.

The posters were designed to catch the eye with their boldness and brightness of color and their cleanness and simplicity of line and legend, whether the viewer saw them from five feet away in a store window or 50 feet away on a billboard in a passing automobile.

There were dozens of lithograph companies that specialized in circus posters, most located in cities with skilled labor like Cincinnati, Buffalo, and Milwaukee. Putting up over 5,000 posters for each location and the circus in town for only one day resulted in the lithograph business being a big deal.

The calliope always appeared at the end of the circus parade playing "Wait Till The Clouds Roll By Jennie." The calliope was steam powered and could be heard miles away.

The circus, which is given credit for many things in American culture, is credited with being first to develop the billboard as an advertising medium. Some of the billboards were really big. A full size lithograph poster sheet was 28"X 42". The circus used every size from a half poster sheet to the rare 100-sheet poster with many sizes in between. Some of these billboards were over 50 feet long and 12 to 15 feet high.

Within a day or two, signs announcing, "the circus is coming to Olean" were just about everywhere; not just nailed to telephone poles, posters appeared in store windows and billboards were covered with posters. Out in the country, posters were pasted on the sides of barns. It seemed like every vacant wall touted the circus. And believe me, these posters were colorful, attention-grabbing and well-done overall. Beautiful acrobats swinging from trapezes in the top of tents, sword swallowers, fat ladies, fire eaters, elephants standing on their hind legs and lions and tigers staring from the center ring cage — all were there.

The general contractor was the first circus employee to cover the route, and he made written contracts for virtually everything needed at each of the circus stops---permits, licenses, exhibition grounds, billboard rentals, water, animal feed and food for the circus employees. As a result, the general contractor was often a fully educated and trained lawyer.

The circus business was very competitive and over 40 circuses were on tour in the 1930's and 40's ,many of them traveling the same routes to the same cities. The circus-advertising machine was a sophisticated operation. A large circus like Ringling Bros would have four advertising railroad cars which followed each other a week or two apart with very specific assignments. Collectively these were known as carriers for the "Advance Men."

These railcars were brightly painted with the name of the circus prominently displayed on the sides. The cars were attached to any convenient passenger train that happened to fit their schedule. Each car contained an office, work area, supply room, and accommodations for the crew who slept in the railcar.

The first car, sometimes known as the "opposition car" or the "skirmishing car," was a troubleshooter. The advance men riding in this car made sure that competing shows did not sabotage previously arranged dates and contracts.

The second railcar arrived about one week later carrying an advance agent, a press agent, and a group of billposters, usually about 16 people. While en-route, at night, the bill posters would be busy preparing the flour and water-based paste, which was used to put the posters up the next day. The number of bills posted varied, of course, but the average was about 5,000 lithographs per locality. The advance agent had to keep track of where these were placed and the number of complimentary tickets issued to obtain permission to put up the posters. These people could transform the landscape of a town in a single day and, when they were finished, you would need to be in a cave not to know "the circus is coming to town." Just imagine, as was often the case, the amount of advertising when more than one circus was arriving in a town in a space of just a few weeks.

The third advance car verified the work of the previous car and made sure the poster bills had not been defaced, destroyed by rain, or covered by a rival or an advertisement for some other product. If a farmer or business owner violated the terms of the billposting contract, the circus simply rescinded his ticket privileges. Compensation for bill posting privileges almost always consisted of free tickets to the circus performance, cash was rarely used.

The press agent assigned to the second car made the initial contact with the usual several daily newspapers in each town. He had a standard, but slightly different press release for each paper. The press people in the third railcar to visit the city, usually a few weeks before the arrival of the circus, took care of circus advertising arrangements with the local papers, and made free tickets available to local reporters, police officers, politicians, and other local dignitaries. This helped arrange positive press coverage, a little extra surveillance on circus day, and a friendly reception around town.

The circus wagons were hand carved in elaborately decorated pieces of art.

The final advance car arrived just ahead of the circus and made a few last minute arrangements for a local drug store or book center to sell tickets and made a final review of all the critical arrangements; the circus route, food, circus exhibit grounds, any required permits, etc..

In a little act of circus puffery, the press agents often submitted false reviews of the show that were unflaggingly positive. Their "after blast" reviews appeared pretty much verbatim in town after town as the circus made its way across

America.

With the posters up, the signs in practically every business window in town, tickets on sale, the exhibition grounds prepared, the circus was ready to come to town. Keep in mind throughout most of the schedule, the circus was only in town for less than a day. This advance process was going on just about seven days a week for the eight months the show traveled.

Now, on my way to and from school, there was a circus poster of some type in just about every store window. Richardson's grocery had several and Duffy's Soda Fountain had a particularly eye-catching one of a scantily clad woman on a flying trapeze--we boys looked at that every day. Outside of town, it was not just billboards that announced the circus, the entire side of barns carried the message in lithographs brighter than I had ever seen. My father would point out articles in the local Times Herald afternoon newspaper that covered exciting elements of the circus. It would be arriving Wednesday morning on four separate trains; one carrying all the animals, including 50 elephants and 40 lions, tigers and panthers.

My father, who worked at the local refinery, was thoroughly thrilled with the circus, my mother not so much. We even drove over to the Jaekle Brothers lot where the circus would be set up. This lot was very close to the center of town and was used as a riding stable most of the year. The reason nothing had ever been built on the property was because it frequently flooded in the spring due to the nearby Olean Creek. Looking at this empty field and seeing it later covered with canvas, 40 tents in all, seemed unbelievable that this could happen overnight.

I know it was dark, probably 5 o'clock in the morning,

when my father woke me and announced to hurry and get dressed, we were going to see the circus train. A very short drive to the railroad yards, and there parked, side by side, were four painted trains –the circus had arrived!

People were busy and there was a lot of activity taking place around the first train--the others were mostly silent, a lot of my friends were already examining the train loaded with the animal cages.

The railroad circus was a complex, but extremely smooth-operating organization. Of course, Ringling Bros. was the largest, consisting of four separate trains, 107 railroad cars each 70 feet long, which was double the normal length at the time. Ringling is given credit for being the first to use the piggy back system of loading one container or wagon on top of another.

In the "Golden Age" of the railroad circus, (1900-1930), a morning parade would take place leaving the rail siding around ten o'clock and arriving at the exhibit grounds, known as "the lot," around 11:00 AM. These parades were wonderful spectacles in small towns with a colorful band in front, followed by the elephants in their trunk to tail form, the wild animals in their cages and the clowns performing their stunts and making mischief along the way. The calliope, a trademark of the circus, always was last in the parade and always played "Wait Till The Clouds Roll By Jennie."

The calliope (ke-lai-ipe) is a musical instrument that produces sound by sending steam or compressed air through large whistles. One thing is certain, calliopes are loud, the sound can be heard for miles, which is why the circus used them. The first calliopes were used on steam riverboats and later it became a fixture at the "tail end" of the circus parade. The calliope was always a beautiful carved, painted, and gilded wagon pulled by two or four handsome workhorses.

It could be played from a keyboard, but more often a mechanical player was used, similar to a roller on a player piano. The typical calliope had 32 whistles, but the number could range from 25 to 67 whistles. Tuning a device of this type and size was extremely difficult and off pitch notes, particularly in the upper register, are a trade mark of the calliope. One manufacturer located in Peru, Indiana, continues to produce the steam calliope—the last builder in the world. A calliope still makes an occasional appearance in major parades around the world.

The circus parade disappeared in the 1930's for a combination of reasons. Cities had grown larger and more congested making the parade route difficult to navigate; circus employees were joining unions, and objecting to many things including long working days; the parade interfered with business and cities began to refuse to issue parade permits; and, as you might expect, lawsuits began to multiply for any mishap along the parade route. So, another grand American institution fell by the wayside with many more to follow as the years sped by.

The social structure of the railroad circus was built upon an occupational hierarchy akin to a caste system, in which musicians ate and slept with musicians, and concession attendants, known as "candy butchers," ate and slept with candy butchers. As a result, in a large circus many of the employees never met each other. The pole setters, stake drivers, and general roustabouts rode in the first car and arrived at the exhibit grounds many hours before the performers, and when the show ended, they were the last to leave. Because workers spent a great deal of time working, eating and sleeping with people performing the same task, they formed very close bonds with each other.

On the circus train single male and female employees occupied separate Pullman cars, while married couples had their own cars. These accommodations were pretty primitive, 64 people per car. There were bunk beds, stacked three high, four washbasins, and four lavatories at the end of each car. Any full-body bathing had to be done in the dressing tent at the grounds before the afternoon show each day. This was not easy since you had to use buckets of icy cold water. Each rail car had a porter who shined shoes, took care of the laundry once a week and kept the berths neat and clean.

The laborers, known as "roustabouts" slept in the stock car or flatcar close to the areas where they worked. The elephant men, and Ringling had 60 elephant handlers, slept in a narrow space above the animals, which meant they were with the elephants virtually non-stop. Bathing was a rare occurrence for the average worker.

Some of the top performers were awarded roomettes on the train or in some rare cases staterooms with twin beds and a private bathroom instead of bunks with facilities at the end of the railcar. Lillian Leitzel, an acrobat, and generally considered the greatest circus star of all time, demanded a private Pullman car and her own lavish dressing tent, and John Ringling gave her both.

The unloading, and 12 hours later, the reloading of these special brightly painted railcars was a marvel to behold. The first train, known as "the flying squadron" was already being rapidly unloaded when Dad and I arrived. This train carried the dining tent and all its equipment and personnel, the "lot" layout crew and stake drivers, sideshow equipment and personnel and the animals for the menagerie. The second train carried the show animals, wardrobe wagons, sleeping quarters for some of the animal keepers and the Big Top with all its rigging. The third train was loaded with all the required seating, lighting, generators, and an assortment of tents for the blacksmith, first aid, maintenance, etc.

The last train carried the performers and the management. John Ringling's private car, named "Jomar," was usually attached to this train. The name Jomar was a combination of the first names of John and his wife Mabel. This private car was 83 feet long with its own kitchen, dining room, bathroom, and two bedrooms. The private railcar was the status symbol of the 1920's and 30's, like the private jet plane today. John's brother, Charles, who was operations manager, also had his own private car, which was a little longer than John's car. "Jomar" is on display in Sarasota, Florida at the Ringling Circus Museum.

Ringling Brothers used four trains and 104 railcars to transport the circus to over 100 cities each year.

JOHN RINGLING

John Ringling ran Ringling Brothers circus from the beginning with five of his seven brothers. This barefoot boy from Baraboo, Wisconsin, son of German immigrants, became one of the wealthiest people in the world.

John Ringling had a few other extravagances in addition to the railcar, including a yacht named Zalphus, five Rolls Royce autos, a house on Fifth Avenue in New York City, a ranch in Montana, and a mansion and large museum for his vast art collection, both in Sarasota, Florida.

John Ringling ran the circus from the beginning with five of his seven brothers. Each brother managed a separate operation of the circus. John was the advance man making all the arrangements and establishing the necessary advertising and publicity. Charles was the operations manager supervising the daily operation of the circus. The brothers began to die in the early 1900's, and by 1926, John was the only brother alive. He began purchasing smaller circuses and by 1929, Ringling had a monopoly in the circus business. John Ringling was also powerful in a host of other fields including owning many small railroads and banks and he was a major player in the short-lived Florida real estate boom of the 1920's.

John Ringling's day-to-day life could be a model for a movie depicting the lifestyle of the rich and famous. Nothing but the very best suited him, whether it be wine or beer, an acrobat's performance, an oil painting, a car, a yacht, or an apple, he loved the utmost in luxury. This extended to eating where every meal was a feast, including breakfast, which he had at three pm each day. Ringling's workday was unusual, 3:00 pm to about 4:00 am. John was a big man and he consumed a breakfast of steak, potatoes, eggs, biscuits, fruit, and more. Finishing the day at four in the morning, he might devour a couple of roast chickens, and up to a dozen pints of beer. John had diabetes and his wife did her best to control his diet, but she had very little success. For example, he outmaneuvered Mabel's attempts to limit his beer consumption by having a refrigerator installed behind a huge nude painting in the basement card room where he entertained his many friends. Guests at Ca'd' Zan (House of John in Italian) during the "Roaring Twenties" included a "Who's Who" of America: Will Rogers, Flo Ziegfeld, Al Smith, John McGraw and dozens more and all their friends. During the height of Prohibition, 1920's, he had an entire ocean freighter full of liquor shipped from Europe to Sarasota where it anchored offshore and the booze was ferried to the estate by small speed boats.

John Ringling was frequently absent from the circus for extended periods of time tending to his many other business interests. Trips to Europe were necessary because one of his main duties was scouting for new talent. It was during these European excursions that John assembled his extensive and extremely valuable art collection. On more than one occasion it took an entire ship to transport his purchases from Port Genoa to Tampa, Florida. In addition to paintings, he brought home a considerable amount of statuary; there are over 1200 statues in the gardens adjacent to Ca'd'Zan. When John did appear on the circus lot it was, of course, always in the afternoon or evening and his main concern was always safety, not just safety for the performers, but safety for the workers, the animals and the audience as well.

Try to picture this scene: always a big cigar, over six feet tall, heavy, not fat, drooping dark eyes, arrogant, egocentric and terribly smart. His memory was colossal. He could easily recall the name of every person who had ever been involved with the circus; this included performers, bankers, food suppliers, even mayors and weather forecasters. He knew every railroad route in America and the economic ups and downs of every city on every route. This is why from the very beginning John was totally in charge of planning the schedule for the upcoming season. He was able to shun the places where money was tight and play the ones where things were going well.

Ca'd'Zan, John Ringling's 56 room mansion in Sarasota, Florida, was completed in 1926. Resembling a Venetian Gothic palace with marble stairs, tapestries and elaborately carved and gilded furniture, the mansion is part of the Ringling Museum, and tours are available daily.

John Ringling was a "big picture" guy, an administrator, but his major liability was an inability to focus on details-- they were beneath him. Rarely did he arrive anywhere on time, not even for the most important meetings, he always kept everyone waiting. He often arranged meetings knowing in advance that he would not attend. Performers and assistants would come to him with requests, and thinking of something else and not paying attention, he would give his "ok"-- and was astounded later to discover what he had approved. All these things were merely details, trifles, of which he was totally contemptuous. This trait of not concerning himself with details, "the little things," served him well and saved a lot of time and needless worry during the years when things were going well; but when the financial crisis hit, it was a major contributor to his downfall.

Jomar, named after John Ringling and his wife Mabel, was the Ringling's private railcar. It was 83 feet long and featured a kitchen, dining room, bathroom, and two bedrooms.

Ca'd'Zan, the Ringling Mansion, was completed in 1926. The over-the-top 56 room winter residence on Sarasota Bay resembles a Venetian Gothic palace. Marble, tapestries and elaborately carved and gilded furniture dominate the interior.

15

Tours are available daily throughout the year.

In 1928, when work was only beginning on the Ringling Art Museum adjacent to the mansion, John Ringling publicly announced his gift of the property to the state of Florida. This had been his dream from the beginning of moving the circus winter quarters to Sarasota.

It is important to understand that this gift involved no deed or signed document. The entire art collection and buildings remained in his name till the day he died. But with a man like John Ringling, when you give your word it is a "done deal". As a result, when the financial crash of 1929 took him to the verge of ruin, and the sale of just a few of the collection's masterpieces would have saved him, he refused to even consider it. This is a guy who began life as a barefoot boy on the bank of the river in Baraboo, Wisconsin; son of poor German immigrants, who made himself one of the wealthiest people in the world, lived like a medieval prince and loved it, yet, ultimately he was willing to risk everything to keep his dream intact. What a man! People who knew him well, Fred Bradna ringmaster for Ringling's for 40 years, his nephew John Ringling North and others loved big John Ringling. He was generous, interesting, exciting and it was just fun to be in his company.

There were over 700 paintings in the museum's collection when it opened and a list of just some of the artists is impressive: Titian, Rembrandt, Frans Hals, Brenghel, El Greco, Velazquez, Goya, Gainsborough, and on and on. Today it boasts the largest collection of Rubens' paintings in the world. This place is definitely worth a visit. In addition to the museum and Ca'd'Zan, the grounds include a circus museum and the largest miniature circus in the world, built entirely by one man, it is simply wonderful.

John's wife Mabel pre-deceased him in 1929, and he was absolutely devastated; however, true to his nature, one year later he married a young, wealthy widow. The marriage was doomed from the beginning with two very similar strong personalities. After two years they were separated and the divorce became final after John's death.

On December 2nd, 1936, still reviewing art catalogues for possible purchases and planning a circus spectacle called "Golden Are The Days of Memory," the giant of the circus died of pneumonia, at age 70, in his home on Park Avenue, New York City.

He had been involved with the circus his whole life, and is credited with most of the innovations we consider standard for a show to be considered a circus.

The stock market crash of 1929 and the collapse of the Florida real estate boom had pretty much wiped out John's fortune. He no longer owned the circus and the Ca'd'Zan mansion was his only major possession.

The "Big Top" was the largest of the 41 tents set up and torn down at each of 107 cities visited annually. The tent accommodated 13,000 people and occupied over two acres.

THE "SET UP'

When they began unloading the "Big Top" from the third train, my father decided we had better head over to the circus grounds and watch them set up this traveling company town. Altogether these four trains, 107 railcars, carried 102 equipment wagons, 55 baggage wagons, 22 animal cages, and three ticket wagons. After watching all this being unloaded from 70 extra-lengths specially designed flat cars in exactly the right order---well, it was easy to understand why the German general staff came over here to study the operation--unfortunately.

Ringling Bros. in an average year visited 137 cities spread across this country and 107 of these visits would be one-night stands and at each they would unload, set-up, tear-down and reload the trains. Imagine the need for order.

The next stop was Jaekle's field on the other side of town to view what the circus called the "set-up." The creation of a small self-contained tent city was already underway and would be completed in about two hours.

A review of a few statistics will give you an idea of the enormous size of this temporary city that appeared and disappeared, without a trace by the way, in about 16 hours. Ringling Bros & Barnum and Bailey Circus required a minimum of ten to 15 acres to accommodate 41 tents. These tents included, in addition to the Big Top, the menagerie tent, sideshow tent, dining tent, cookhouse tent, three dressing tents, an equestrian tent for the horses, on down to the barber's tent, medical tent, harness tent, and blacksmith tent.

When Dad and I arrived, the Dining Tent was already up and the 174 cooks, waiters, butchers, bakers, and busboys were swinging into action. At 7:30 am, the flag went up and the loudspeakers announced, "Ham and eggs, hotcakes, come and get em." By ten o'clock, the bulk of the 1500 circus personnel had been served and the "cook tent" began to prepare for lunch.

The "cook tent" was always the first tent to appear on the lot and it was a marvel of efficiency. The entire operation was self-sufficient, including stoves, ovens, refrigerators, and dishwashers. The "advance man" had made arrangements for local suppliers to provide the fresh food required weeks ahead-- everything else needed was supplied by the circus.

The circus caste system was very evident in the dining tent. The tent had two separate entrances and was divided down the center by a curtain. Laborers, roustabouts, and animal attendants ate on one side and management and performers dined on the other side. The owner's table was at the front of the tent followed by show managers and star acts. Secondary performers sat in the rear of the tent. Each occupation had its own table. Even the bands were separated into the Big Top band, the after-show concert band, and the lowest class sideshow band. The managers and stars ate in groups at small tables, while the others ate at long tables. The folks at the top had table settings of china, while the rest used enameled tinplate. Everyone had an assigned seat and was served by a staff of waiters, each handling about 20 diners. By the end of the day, they would have served over 5,000 meals using 4,000 pounds of meat, 4500 eggs, and 2,000 gallons of coffee. A typical breakfast would consume 5,000 pancakes.

these people were hard workers and hungry.

The cook tent was always the first to appear on the lot, and it was also the first to leave and be packed on the train. As soon as the last person finished dinner, usually about 6:30 P.M., the laborers poured onto the site packing all the equipment into crates, dishes, and food into boxes, pulling the tent stakes and folding the canvas. Everything had to be organized so that 12 hours later the entire process could be repeated in the next town----train unloaded, tent set-up, equipment unpacked, tables and chairs arranged in exactly the correct order and another 5,000 meals served.

The "Big Top Gang" was composed of 175 canvas men. By the time this group arrived on the show grounds, the layout crew of 41 men had driven stakes with small white flags attached into the ground designating where every major tent pole should be placed. The Big Top was 510 feet long and 210 feet wide and accommodated over 12,000 people. Visualize this tent, 200 feet longer than a football field and three times as wide. It's a wonder anyone in the cheap seats saw anything. Inside the tent, there were three circus rings, each 42 feet in diameter, and four stages between the rings. The diameter of a circus ring was established over 200 years ago as the minimum size needed for a horse to canter in a circle with a rider standing on its back.

Five center poles, placed down the centerline, supported the tent. Each of these poles was over 70 feet long and weighed about a ton. The 74 quarter poles placed around the tent perimeter were each 37 and a half feet long and weighed 600 pounds each. It took a crew of eight men to raise each quarter pole.

Once the center poles were in place, the two and one-half acres of canvas was spread out on the ground and laced together. This enormous blanket of heavy canvas was fastened to rings on the poles and pulled to the top of each pole. In the early days of the circus this herculean task was performed by the elephants and manual labor. Beginning around 1930 pulleys attached to tractors replaced the elephants. Once the quarter poles were in place the guy ropes which stretched from the sidewall poles to the ground had to be secured by countless stakes, each driven into the ground by manual labor.

Overall, the 41 tents used 74 miles of rope. Eight hundred stake locations had been spotted by the layout crew using iron pins topped with small white or red flags. Crews of seven men, each with a 16-pound sledgehammer, pounded a stake four to five feet long and two and one-half inches thick, three feet into the ground at each pin site. As soon as the boss canvas man shouted "down stake" the crew moved to the next iron pin and drove another stake three feet into the ground. A few hours of this labor each day will keep you in pretty good shape.

I spent one college summer working with a railroad "section gang" replacing the wooden ties under the rails. The work required pulling the spikes out of the old ties, using a huge pair of tongs to pull the old ties out from under the rails, replacing them with new ties and securing the rails to the new ties with spikes about six inches long. Skill was needed to drive the spike into the tie without damaging the rail with an errant blow of the sledgehammer. I was 18 years old at the time and the lesson I learned that summer was no matter what happens I must finish college because I never want to work this hard again. I had a very similar experience a few years later when I visited an operating coalmine.

Once the tent was up, which took about two hours, the

crews began erecting the chairs and bleachers to accommodate the 12,000 customers for each of the two performances. The "doors" to the menagerie tent and the "Big Top" opened at 1:00 pm and the matinee performance began at 2:15pm.

Since the circus had 41 tents, a lot of activity had to be going on simultaneously, so by noon the circus lot was a beehive of activity. First, there were about 1,500 circus employees, including 185 performers, and each and every one was doing something. The blacksmith was shoeing horses, the harness maker was repairing various leather contraptions, the barber was busy in his tent, and the mailman was on his rounds.

Next, we have the animals, including wild animals. Some of these animals will be performers in the Big Top, including 50 elephants, 20 lions and tigers, 40 horses, camels, and an assortment of dogs and monkeys; others will appear only in the menagerie. Some were extra special, such as Gargantua, the famous gorilla.

As the matinee show time arrived, there were 12,000 in the Big Top audience and thousands more milling around outside, exploring the menagerie, visiting the sideshow, or wandering around the lot. I assure you that a lad ten years old from Olean, New York, had never experienced a crowd this large before.

In the midst of all this activity, the 185 performers including clowns, acrobats, animal trainers, aerialists, and ballet girls, had to prepare to put on the "show of a lifetime." Certain circus backlot customs had endured for over 100 years and the social structures or caste system was one of them. The preferred accommodations on the rail car, the upfront seating in the dining tent, this preferred placement based on rank in the circus extended to the dressing tents. The stars had their trunks and water buckets placed nearest the entrance, while lesser lights, such as ballet girls, were way in the back of the tent. Since there was no running water on the circus lot, each performer was allotted two buckets of water for the day. These buckets had the person's name on them and were placed in the exact same location in the tent each day.

Performers were also allowed two trunks, one for costumes, and one for personal effects. The circus had 65 people assigned to the task of handling these trunks and water buckets. If a particular costume for a general act, such as the finale, was supplied by the circus, the performer obtained it from the wardrobe tent. The dressing tents were attached to the Big Top entrance and the wardrobe tent was attached to the rear of the dressing tents.

LILLIAN LEITZEL

Lillian Leitzel, considered the greatest circus star of all time was Ringling's headline attraction for 15 years beginning in 1920. Her act, known as the "plange turn," involved being hoisted to the top of the tent hanging from a swiveled rope.

A few super stars, very few, have always had their own private dressing tent and their private stateroom on the train. The first performer to succeed in convincing management to provide them with their own exclusive dressing tent was Lillian Leitzel, considered the greatest circus star of all time. Lillian Leitzel commanded a pre-eminence never attained by another circus star. She was a prima donna of the greatest magnitude and was later emulated by many of the Hollywood super stars.

Lillian Leitzel was born in 1892 in Breslau, Germany to a family of circus performers. She was well educated and had prepared for a career as a concert pianist, but joined her mother's circus group and became an accomplished acrobat. The group came to the United States in 1910 and she was spotted by an agent of Ringling Bros. in 1914.

Leitzel's act featured feats of endurance performed on the Roman Rings. John Ringling adored her and through a combination of advertising, showmanship and publicity turned her into the biggest star of the 1920's; she was in a class by herself. Her entrance to the center ring was a classic in circus showmanship. The entire Big Top was dark. The band was quiet; one spotlight illuminated the edge of the ring. This tiny figure stood poised at the edge, she was four-feet nine inches tall and weighed 94 pounds, crowned by a pile of blonde hair.

She was always accompanied by a six-foot, four-inch footman and a maid who stood at the edge of the ring for the entire performance. On muddy days, the footman carried Leitzel into the arena.

Once aloft, at the very top of the tent, Leitzel performed for six minutes on two rings, eight inches in diameter. No matter what gymnastic feat she performed, it was perfect and it looked so easy anyone could do it. Throughout the act, she would be smiling and blowing kisses to the thousands of upturned faces. No other acts would be competing with her in the other two rings.

At the conclusion of this act, she descended to the ring, bowed to the crowd, and was pulled aloft on a swiveled rope upon which she did her specialty, technically known as the "plange turn." With her right hand and wrist in a rope loop attached to a swivel, she swung her body up to the level of her shoulder, hesitated momentarily, then threw her body up and over until she was hanging by her wrist again. Leitzel could do this feat an incredible number of times, once establishing a record of 249 turns. For the act, she eventually limited herself to 60 turns and kept the audience's attention by involving them in the count---48, 49, 50... She was constantly being treated for rope burns, strains, and sprains; when the pain became too much, she would switch the act to her left hand.

This was not a pretty act or a graceful act, but it was an act of breathtaking endurance and strength by a charming four-foot nine-inch, cute little lady who really knew how to capture an audience. Leitzel had learned the act from her mother at the age of 11.

For fourteen consecutive years, Lillian Leitzel remained the undisputed star of "The Greatest Show on Earth." She was very conscious of her position and was a wizard at using her status to gain favors from management.

More than any other performer, Miss Leitzel was responsible for the great improvement that changed performer's living accommodations from truly sordid to sumptuous.

Every star that followed Leitzel owed her a debt of thanks.

Leitzel persuaded Ringling Bros. to provide her with, not just a stateroom on the train, but an entire Pullman car and a grand piano. In addition, she was the first to have her own private dressing tent. This sumptuous tent had its own awning-shaded piazza where she would usually entertain the top members of the circus and just about every dignitary of the town the circus was visiting. Travelling from coast to coast with her private railcar and absolutely lavish dressing tent, she undoubtedly met and entertained every U.S. Senator, financial magnate, union boss, and anyone else of importance in America. She even kept Henry Ford and his bouquet of roses waiting outside her tent. It is possible that no other star in any endeavor has reached the level of preeminence gained by Miss Lillian Leitzel.

Leitzel's personality seemed to be divided into two totally separate spheres. Professionally her quick temper was legendary. It was not uncommon to see her cursing and slapping a roustabout who did not adjust the rigging to her liking. She would frequently fly off the handle and fire her long-time personal maid, Mabel Cummings, re-hiring her in the same day.

The private side of Miss Leitzels's personality was the direct opposite of the professional side. She was charming, she was kind, the perfect hostess, especially since she was fluent in three languages. She was especially thrilled by children and would gather them about her between shows and tell them stories and play Mozart, Chopin, and Schumann on her baby grand piano. She would often be on the floor giving piggyback rides or doing other stunts that horrified management lest she get injured. She never missed hosting birthday parties for fellow performers' children. Although married at least three times, some didn't count. Leitzel never had any children.

Naturally she was pursued by many wealthy, and some famous suitors. She was married first to a minor circus stagehand. She always claimed she couldn't remember his name and referred to him as "what's-his-name." Next came Clyde Ingalls, the circus sideshow manager who couldn't tolerate all the attention she continued to receive and they divorced quickly. Leitzel liked to help the Ringling's engender goodwill for the circus by entertaining the rich and powerful in her dressing tent. A wealthy Chicago sportsman returned the favor by throwing a huge party at the Stevens Hotel, now the Conrad Hilton, in downtown Chicago-one of the largest hotels in the world at the time. There was a display featuring a mermaid swimming in a tank of vintage champagne, and a gold- plated statue of Leitzel as the centerpiece. The host passed out $50.00 bills to each of the guests, remember this is 1921; Leitzel received a diamond tiara that one guest observed was worth only slightly less than the hotel. Ingalls' jealousy passed the point of no return and the marriage was over. Finally, the circus trapeze performer Alfredo Codona, in 1928, arrived on the scene. Even today, Alfredo Codona is considered the greatest trapeze artist, known as flyers in the circus world, of all time. He was absolutely brilliant at his craft, the first to perform the elusive triple somersault consistently, perfect technique to a level of graceful aerial ballet. Codona was the product of a circus family in Mexico and actually participated with his father and brothers in a trapeze act beginning at age five. Codona married a fellow-flyer from Cincinnati, Ohio in 1917 and divorced ten years later. By the time, he encountered

Lillian Lietzel he had developed into one of the brightest stars under the Big Top. Codona was not only a superb trapeze artist; he was the handsomest man in the circus; lean, muscular, dark, jet-black hair, and of course, in perfect condition.

The circus publicity department made sure the entire world knew of the romance between the king and queen of the circus. Once again, things did not last because Codona's Latin blood could not take the adulation Leitzel continued to receive, and Leitzel could not even begin to abandon the worship heaped upon her by the masculine world.

After three years of a roller coaster marriage alternating between idyllic romance and furious clashes of temperament, they separated. In the winter of 1931, Leitzel was touring Europe on the vaudeville circuit when in Copenhagen, Denmark at the height of her act the brass swivel on her performing rope had crystallized and snapped. She fell to the stage floor on her head and shoulder. This was about a distance of 20 feet. Stunned, but apparently not injured, she attempted to return to the act but was overruled and sent to a hospital. Codona, who was performing in Berlin, rushed to her side and the next day they returned together to Berlin. Two days later she died of an apparent concussion at the age of 39. Codona died six years later, killing his then-current wife at the time, equestrienne Vera Bruce, and himself with a revolver. He is buried next to Leitzel, the love of his life, in Inglewood, California. Codona had a 12- foot high marble statue constructed at the burial site that depicts Leitzel and him in a flying embrace, like angels.

TOM THUMB

The wedding of Livinia Warren and Tom Thumb, February 10, 1863 remains one of the highlights in New York City history.

The first really large tent at the show grounds was the sideshow tent. The "Sideshow," known as the "kid show" within the circus community, and often called the "freak show," had its own separate identity among circus folks. Members of the sideshow travelled in a separate railcar, ate before the other performers in the "cookhouse" or dining tent, and generally "kept to themselves" in a special area of the backlot on the grounds. Performers in the "Big Top" rarely knew anyone associated in any way with the Sideshow, which usually had about 40 performers, a 12 to 14 piece band, a complete minstrel show, and a family of midgets.

This particular day the show consisted of 17 acts ranging from six midgets, including four from the Doll family, to a sword swallower, comedy jugglers, and, of course, the "fat lady." Other oddities included the "Rubber Armed Man," Female Hercules, Upside Down Artist, and the Fire Eater. All these marvels were displayed across the front of the tent on large canvas banners. These were very colorful displays, each eight feet wide and 20 feet high. There was one banner for each act and in total the colorful display was known as the "banner line."

In the center of the banner line, a large stage held the very professional announcer flanked by two ticket sellers. The show was open continuously, even during the Big Top performance and you could enter and leave the sideshow tent at any time. To attract customers one of the featured attractions was always performing out front on the stage behind the announcer.

Almost from the beginning of the circus in America, management had found some sort of sideshow, separate from the main event, to be an especially profitable operation. The typical circus sideshow, and there are also sideshows with carnivals, had three distinct elements: strange people, strange animals, and entertainers. Phineas T. Barnum (P.T. Barnum), 1810 to 1891, was undoubtedly the most famous exhibitor of freaks in American history.

Barnum had many, many great acts but the best was probably General Tom Thumb, actually, Charles S. Stratton of Bridgeport, Connecticut, a perfectly formed midget 32inches tall and weighing 33 pounds. P.T. Barnum's fascination with freaks and their exploitation for profit was not based on the fact they were deformed, but on the basis that they were unique and Tom Thumb was the perfect example.

The wedding of Tom Thumb and Lavinia Warren in 1863 was certainly one of the great exploitations in America's history. She was exactly Tom Thumb's height, 32 inches, and weighed 29 pounds. The wedding took place at Grace Church in New York City, Tuesday, February 10, 1863. It remains to this day one of the major moments, and there are many, in New York history.

In the months, leading up to the wedding Barnum's New York City museum where Tom Thumb was appearing was grossing $3,000 a day and the lines were always around the block. Barnum asked the couple to delay the wedding a month but they refused.

Tom Thumb was 25 years old and his bride was 22. The guest list included 2,000 representatives, of what the New York Times called "the elite, the crème de la crème, the upper team, the select few, the very powers of the city — nay of the country." There were members of Congress, governors of several states, the Astors, the Vanderbilts, and the Belmonts. This wedding was taking place at the height of the Civil War and Major General Ambrose E. Burnside represented the Army of the Potomac. Broadway closed from ninth to twelfth streets and an immense crowd had gathered before dawn hoping for a glimpse of the bride and groom.

The wedding was scheduled to take place at noon and Lavinia's carriage arrived right on time to great cheers from the immense crowd. A three-foot high platform was erected before the altar so the bride and groom could see and be seen.

Miss Minnie Warren, Lavinia's 25-inch tall sister, was maid of honor and Commodore Nutt, another midget employee of Barnum's, was best man. He was the son of a New Hampshire farmer and measured 29 inches tall and weighed 24 pounds. The wedding reception at the Metropolitan Hotel was attended by 10,000, with thousands more gathered in the street outside the hotel.

The next day the couple set off on their honeymoon, which included a visit to the White House complete with a Presidential dinner and reception attended by numerous dignitaries, cabinet ministers, senators, and congressmen. President Lincoln, who was six- feet, four- inches tall, was especially interested in Lavinia (according to gossip of the time, she bore a remarkable facial resemblance to his wife, Mary Todd Lincoln). It is reported that on this visit Tom Thumb, "General Tom Thumb," advised Lincoln that his friend Barnum could end the war in a month.

Barnum continued to manage the couple and they made frequent trips to Europe where Tom Thumb was extremely popular, especially with the British Royal Family, Queen Victoria and the young Prince of Wales.

Under Barnum's management, Tom Thumb became a wealthy man owning a house in the fashionable part of New York and a steam yacht. When Barnum eventually got into financial difficulties, Tom Thumb bailed him out and they became business partners. Tom Thumb was tiny in size but he had a quick wit, which helped his popularity, and a very agile mind for business affairs.

Tom Thumb died of a sudden stroke at age 45 and Barnum had a life-size statue erected at the gravesite in Bridgeport, Connecticut. Some years later Lavinia married an Italian Count, a midget who had made a fortune touring as Count Rosebud. When she died, 35 years after Tom, she was buried beside him with the simple inscription "His Wife."

Tom Thumb shown with P.T. Barnum, was actually Charles S. Stratton of Bridgeport, Connecticut, a perfectly formed midget 32 inches tall and weighing 33 pounds.

Jumbo was the most successful circus attraction in history. He was 12 feet tall and weighed 13,000 pounds. Jumbo's brief career ended when he was struck by a train in St. Thomas, Ontario, Canada.

JUMBO

P.T. Barnum's promotional skills were not limited to humans; he is also credited with the promotion of the elephant known as "Jumbo." The promotion of Jumbo was undoubtedly Barnum's greatest single achievement in the world of the circus, and it still stands today as the best and the biggest promotion in circus history. It was even bigger and better than the ballyhoo of the gorilla "Gargantua" or the "Living Unicorn" almost a century later.

Jumbo had been captured as a baby in Ethiopia by a band of Arabs and was sold to the Paris zoo. The Paris zoo had plenty of elephants and wanted a rhinoceros. The London zoo needed an elephant, so they worked out a trade.

When Jumbo arrived in London, he was found to be severely ill. A keeper named Matthew Scott, "Scotty," nursed him back to health and the two became inseparable. Jumbo grew and grew and reached a height of 12 feet and weighed 13,000 pounds. He could reach an object 26 feet from the ground with his 7-foot trunk. But he was most famous for his gentleness and literally hundreds of thousands of children had ridden in the "howdah" strapped to his back as he plodded the gravel paths of the London zoo for 16 years. He was undeniably the number one zoo attraction and the people and the press loved him.

Famous people from Theodore Roosevelt to the young

Winston Churchill were photographed with Jumbo, and P.T. Barnum had visited him several times. Barnum knew that Jumbo, the largest animal in captivity at the time, would be perfect for the circus. Barnum offered $10,000 for the elephant, and it took only two days for the directors of the zoo to decide to accept the offer. The zoo officials had two private reasons for agreeing to sell Britain's favorite pet. First, Jumbo was nearing adulthood, a time when male elephants experience a condition called "musth" which raises their testosterone levels by as much as 60 times causing them to become violent. The other problem was Jumbo's attachment to the keeper "Scotty." When Scotty would leave for the night, the elephant would often throw a tantrum and practically destroy the elephant house. The directors reasoned that Scotty would not be around forever and Jumbo could pose a really big problem. A two- year- old child might throw a tantrum in a playpen, or worse at church, and the worst damage is a little embarrassment, a seven- ton elephant having a temper tantrum is a different event-- walls actually come down.

When the announcement of the sale was made the protests swept throughout Britain all the way from the King and Queen to the thousands of schoolchildren who had grown to love the animal. For P.T. Barnum, the master showman, this was just perfect. In fact, he put some of his publicists to work in England fanning the protest movement against selling the elephant. His shrewd reasoning figured that getting the British to complain about what they were losing was the surest way to make Americans appreciate what they were getting. The public outcry included a nationwide schoolchildren letter writing campaign protesting the sale. To fan the protest flames even more, Jumbo initially refused to board the ship for America sparking another huge protest in the British press.

Despite all the uproar, on March 15, 1882, Jumbo was hoisted aboard the Assyroase Monarch along with his keeper Matthew Scott whom Barnum had wisely hired. Two weeks later the ship docked in New York and Jumbo, still in his special crate, was hoisted ashore onto a special wagon. New York officials and the public wanted Jumbo to parade up Broadway to Madison Square Garden but Barnum was afraid that something would frighten the elephant and he might attack the crowd. There were already 10,000 on-lookers crowding the dock hoping for a glimpse of the famous animal. Eight horses and 500 men could not budge the wagon. Another eight horses and two Asian elephants from the circus were needed to get the wagon moving. When he reached Madison Square Garden, the largest crowd in circus history at the afternoon performance welcomed Jumbo. Jumbo had arrived in New York City on Easter Sunday, just in time for the Madison Square Garden opening of the Greatest Show on Earth. The dollars and cents arithmetic demonstrates the skill of Barnum. Jumbo had cost $30,000 to buy and bring to America. In the first six weeks in this country Jumbo's appearance grossed $336,000.

Jumbo turned out to be the most successful circus attraction in history; but he only lived three and a half more years. Jumbo went on the annual tour with the Greatest Show on Earth in his own private railroad car known as "Jumbo's Palace Car." It was a specially designed boxcar with double doors in the center and painted a bold crimson and gold. Scotty rode in a compartment near Jumbo's head separated by a small door. As long as Scotty was nearby Jumbo's behavior was docile; however, Jumbo never permitted Scotty to close that little door and each day they "shared" a quart of beer together before retiring for the night.

Apparently, a very true story involves Scotty finishing the nightly beer and falling sound asleep without sharing with Jumbo. The elephant wrapped his seven- foot trunk around Scotty, hoisted him in the air, and plunked him down next to the empty beer bottle. Scotty got the message. Whenever Jumbo appeared to be getting sick, Scotty would give him a gallon or two of whiskey. Barnum, a teetotaler, claimed it was stunting the elephant's growth.

Scotty and Jumbo made this 8,000-mile, one-hundred-city tour for the next three years. Jumbo got top billing and became more popular each year as Barnum increased the promotion and the publicity.

On September 15, 1885, the circus was playing in St. Thomas, Ontario, Canada, a small town half way between Buffalo and Detroit. About halfway through the night performance, the 31 circus elephants concluded their final appearance of the night and 29 were taken back to the railroad yards and loaded on the train. The remaining two elephants were needed for the closing act—the smallest, a dwarf clown elephant, appropriately named "Tom Thumb"' and, of course, the largest elephant, Jumbo.

In order to facilitate loading the circus animals on the railcars lined up in a nearby railyard, circus workers had removed a section of chain link fence. The elephants passed over several sets of rails to reach the circus train. As the last elephants, Jumbo and Tom Thumb, crossed the tracks, an unscheduled freight train came roaring down the tracks at full speed since it was not due to stop in St. Thomas. When the engineer spotted the two elephants on the tracks, he blew three blasts on the whistle and threw the train in reverse. The whistle alerted Scotty, and he and the elephants began to run. Tom Thumb's dwarf legs could not keep up and he was the first to be hit breaking his leg and tossing him aside. This saved his life. The train could not stop and as it neared Scotty and Jumbo, Scotty was able to jump between cars on an adjacent track. Jumbo could not react that quickly and was struck from behind carrying him 300 feet down the track and killing him almost instantly. He was 24 years old and Scotty had been by his side for the past 20 years. Both the locomotive and the tender were thrown off the tracks and destroyed beyond repair. Today in St. Thomas, Ontario a life-size statue commemorates Jumbo's tragic end.

P.T. Barnum received the news in New York and, of course, announced how saddened he was and what a financial blow this was to the circus, losing its "superstar." He immediately sued the railroad but settled for a minor amount because he needed the railroad to move his circus around Canada, and railroads were politically powerful at the time.

More importantly, Barnum's imaginative mind swung into action and he told the press, "Long ago I learned that to those who mean right and try their best to do right, there are no such things as real misfortunes. On the other hand, to such persons all apparent evils are blessings in disguise."

The first step Barnum took to turn this tragedy into a "blessing in disguise" was to publish his own version of Jumbo's death. In Barnum's version, Jumbo turned to face the oncoming train, snatched Tom Thumb from in front of the locomotive and hurled the little dwarf elephant 20 yards to safety. Jumbo sacrificed himself to save his best little friend.

Millions of Americans, many who had never seen him, mourned Jumbo's loss as if they had lost a beloved pet and they preferred to accept Barnum's version of his death. As Winston Churchill once said about King Arthur, "It's all true, or it ought to be." A special edition of a children's book, fully illustrated and featuring Jumbo's heroic feat in saving Tom Thumb, was published just before Christmas, 1885.

The next step was to bring Alice, the old female elephant at the London Zoo, to America and bill her as Jumbo's widow in mourning. The circus posters showed Alice and Tom Thumb alongside Jumbo's stuffed carcass. The truth, of course, was that although Alice and Jumbo were in the London Zoo together, neither ever showed any interest whatsoever in the other.

A taxidermist from Rochester, New York, stuffed Jumbo's hide and on instructions from Barnum stretched the hide so the elephant was a foot taller than he actually was in real life.

In the final step, Barnum created a finale for the elephant act that involved the 30 circus elephants sitting and wiping their eyes with large black-bordered, white handkerchiefs.

Barnum, who was a founding trustee and served on the board of Tufts University in Boston, donated the stuffed remains to the school's natural-history museum in 1889, where it remained the centerpiece of the museum, now known as Barnum Hall, until it was destroyed by a fire in 1975. In 2014, the school unveiled a life-size bronze statue of Jumbo on the main quad of the campus and the elephant continues his role as the school mascot. Perhaps Jumbo's most enduring legacy is the word "Jumbo" becoming a part of the English language as a frequently used synonym for anything exceptionally large.

One of the best elephant acts debuted in the spring of 1942 when Ringlings' opened at Madison Square Garden. The program listed "Display No. 18: The Ballet of the Elephants."

50 elephants and 50 beautiful girls in an Original Tour de Force, directed by George Balanchine, with music by Igor Stravinsky. Costumes by Norman Bel Geddes. Elephants trained by Walter McClain. At this time Igor Stravinsky, George Balanchine and Norman Bel Geddes were at the top of their professional careers in their respective fields of music, ballet, and design.

The elephants wore pink tutus and cupcake hats and performed their steps in a golden spotlight. Critics commented on the dancing elephants: "Their deliberate way of kneeling on slow sliding forelegs—like a cat's yawning stretch or a ship's slide into the water is fine ballet."

The Bella ballerina on opening night was Vera Zorina, the dancer and film star, who was married to George Balanchine. In all, there were 425 performances of the circus ballet and the music, called "Circus Polka," continues to be played today.

Some people consider "The Long Mount" the most awesome spectacle of all the traditional circus acts. All 50 elephants come out of the rings, gather around the hippodrome track in single file, and move at once to the front side. Each elephant stands on its hind legs and puts its forelegs on the back of the elephant in front of it. After taking a few paces and waving their trunks to the audience, the act concludes by the trainers and the 50 elephants racing at full gallop out the back door of the tent. The sound resembles a thunderstorm and actually shakes some auditoriums. The display is considered the "kick line" of the circus.

It was announced recently that elephants will no longer be a part of the Ringling Brothers circus acts. After 150 years, the elephant is disappearing from the circus the way the freaks left the sideshow. It will be hard to imagine a circus without an elephant. As P.T. Barnum said, "When entertaining the public it's best to have an elephant." The public's attitude has changed and the elephant is not the curiosity it was in the last century.

Many cities and counties in the U.S. have passed ordinances forbidding elephant acts and even prohibiting circuses completely. It is becoming difficult for Feld Entertainment to schedule the two divisions of the Ringling Bros. Circus, which today visit 115 cities each year.

Eleven elephants currently tour with the circus and it costs $65,000 yearly to care for each one. So the elephants are being permanently retired to Ringling's 200-acre Center for Elephant Conservation located in Polk City, between Orlando and Tampa, Florida. They will be joining 29 elephants on the property now, two others are on breeding loans to zoos. An ongoing research program at the Center is attempting to determine why cancer is much less common in elephants than in humans. Elephants have 20 copies of a cancer-suppressing gene, page 53, while humans have only one copy. The gene helps damaged cells repair themselves or self-destruct when exposed to a cancer causing substance.

The elephant is truly an amazing animal and it is true that the animal has a long memory. Zoologists will tell you that the elephant is second only to the chimpanzee in animal kingdom intelligence. An elephant learns tricks quickly and easily and remembers them forever---long after performing them regularly.

There are two kinds of elephants, African and Asian. The Africans are larger and more difficult to train. In Asia elephants have been used for centuries as work animals, and this undoubtedly accounts for their reliability and comparative gentleness. In addition to being Asian, almost all circus elephants are female since once each year males enter a period known as "musth," when they can act practically insane and become very dangerous.

The elephant's trunk is much more than just a curious appendage. It is so sensitive it can pick up a pin or a peanut with its tip, or it can wrap it around a showgirl and deposit her on its back, or lift a tent pole upright. On the other hand, if angry, the elephant can use the trunk to smash a human being or another animal to a pulp. The elephant is, indeed, king of the jungle.

African elephants are much larger than the Asian species and can weigh up to 15,000 pounds and reach a height over 13 feet. The pregnancy for elephants is 22 months, and at birth, an elephant already weighs over 200 pounds and is about three feet tall. It is easy to distinguish between the two types since the African elephants' ears are much larger. Female elephants tend to live in family groups consisting of one female with her calves or several related females with offspring. The "matriarch," usually the oldest female, leads the groups. The calves are the center of attention in these family groups and rely on their mother's for as long as three years. Males leave after puberty and live by themselves or with other males. Elephants can live up to 70 years in the wild.

Elephants have been a mainstay in the circus since the beginning.

THE SIDESHOW

A few other sideshow acts deserve mention because they became famous at the time, although, thank goodness, today we consider this exploitation of the unfortunate shameful.

Chang and Eng were born joined at the breastbone in Bangkok, Siam (now Thailand) in 1811 and arrived in the U.S. in 1829. The great showman P.T. Barnum began "exhibiting" them as the Siamese twins at his New York City Museum. They became one of the greatest attractions of all time. The twins were on stage over four hours a day, six days a week, performing an assortment of physical stunts including somersaults and backflips. Chang and Eng were also quite smart and spoke English very well. Part of their act involved playing chess with members of the audience and usually winning. After ten years, they retired from show business to a plantation in North Carolina where they met and married the two daughters of a poor white sharecropper.

The twins purchased separate homes and spent half of each week in each house. Try to imagine how this arrangement was able to produce 21 children; Chang had 11 and Eng had 10. Things seemed to work out very well from the beginning since the first two children were born only six days apart. Imagine these children growing up in Mt. Airy, N.C., Asian, and their father and uncle permanently joined at the chest. Many of the descendants of this unique marriage have been very successful in America including a President of the Union Pacific Railroad, an Army Major General and a host of prominent politicians, judges, and college professors.

Following the Civil War, Chang, and Eng lost most of their fortune and they had to return to the carnival and circus circuit. Chang, always surly and ill-tempered, became a heavy drinker. Eng, just the opposite, sweet and always pleasant, a teetotaler, began to play poker far into the night and quarrels were frequent. In addition, the wives were no longer friendly and there were days with no speaking. They began spending thousands of dollars consulting the best doctors in both America and Europe, but since they shared several major organs nothing could be done about separating them.

One morning in 1874, Eng woke up to find Chang had died. Eng called for his wife and began to cry that he was doomed. Doctors were summoned, but Eng died three hours later. They were 63 years old. Both an award-winning novel and a play, which continues to tour Asia, were produced chronicling their unique lives. Once again, a circus word or phrase became part of the English language; Siamese twins describe two humans joined at birth.

Another featured act was the Doll Family, a quartet of four midgets from Germany. Out of a family of seven children, three girls and a boy were midgets, and the other three were average size. The Doll Family became very well-known because, in addition to being tiny, they were very talented performers. The Dolls toured with the circus for 30 years, including 20 continuous years with Ringling Bros, until 1956.

Because of their many talents, including gymnastics, dancing and acting, the Dolls racked up quite an impressive number of movie film credits and were known for a while as

"The Movie Film Midgets." Their most well-known film, and there were many, was probably "The Wizard of Oz" in 1939.

The family retired together and the four of them lived in a large house in Sarasota, Florida. The last survivor of the family was Tiny who died at the age of 90 in September 2004.

After Jumbo and Gargantua the third most famous and controversial animal in circus history turned out to be the "Living Unicorn", or actually four living unicorns. When the circus opened at Madison Square Garden in 1987, a barrage of TV spots showing a creature called "The Living Unicorn" preceded it.

Unicorns are mentioned in Greek mythology as far back as 300 BC, and they are mentioned frequently in the Bible. Many examples of unicorns appear in Roman architecture and throughout history there are references to the unicorn's single horn having mystical powers and drinking from the horn to ward off a host of illnesses. Uni is "one" in Latin, and "corner" means "horn", hence "unicorn." In the early 16th century, medieval art produced a series of seven tapestries showing hunters capturing and killing a unicorn who is ultimately resurrected and shown sitting in a corral representing heaven. Christians believed in the unicorn version of things and it came to symbolize Christ, the horn the Cross. The tribulations during the hunt were like Christ's tribulations on earth.

All this had been going on for over two thousand years and no one had ever seen a living unicorn. All of a sudden in 1985, Ringling Bros comes to town announcing they have four "Living Unicorns."

First, the Society for the Prevention of Cruelty to Animals (SPCA) entered the scene charging these pure animals were really horn-altered goats. This resulted in investigations by several state and federal agencies. The New York Times devoted a full column to a FDA report that had examined the creatures and found them to be one-horned goats. But the FDA reported, they are healthy, well cared for goats. All three major networks entered the debate with appearances on Good Morning America, the Johnny Carson Tonight Show, and CBS News. Even New York Mayor Ed Koch, quite a showman himself, entered the dispute on the side of the circus charging, goats or not, it would be a shame to destroy the fantasy of the "Unicorn."

Things really heated up when the circus, not content with all the free publicity, ran a full-page ad in the New York Times, which read, "Children of all ages believe in Santa Claus, Peter Pan, the Wizard of Oz, and the fabled Unicorn---"DON'T LET THE GRINCHES STEAL THE FANTASY."

The State of New York Consumer Protection Board called on the circus to cease and desist, its promotion of the unicorn. Old P.T. Barnum would have really loved this episode; the circus stayed in New York City for two months and sales increased 55 percent over the prior year.

The four unicorns were in fact Angora goats from northern California sold to the circus by their naturalists owners. Shortly after birth, in a painless procedure, each kid's horn buds were surgically moved to the center of its forehead and fused together, so that a single horn would grow. The creatures had already appeared at San Francisco's Renaissance Fair without creating any controversy. It took New York City and the old circus "ballyhoo" to turn it into the biggest news of the day. The four "unicorns" or goats traveled with the circus for two years and they were the hit of the show.

ADDED NOTE: Shel Silverstein, well known author of

children's books, wrote the lyrics for "The Unicorn", made famous in 1968 by the popular Canadian band "The Irish Rovers." The first verse is as follows: "A long time ago when the Earth was green, There was more kinds of animals than you've ever seen; And they'd run around free when the Earth was born – And the loveliest of 'em all was the unicorn."

Subsequent verses describe Noah building the Ark and the unicorn as the only animal that was playing and hiding and "missed the boat."

The final line of the last verse reads "And that's why you'll never see a unicorn to this very day."

The song was immediately popular, selling millions of copies and remains one of "The Irish Rovers'" all-time major hits, and is popular today in Irish Pubs around the world.

Of all the weirdos and freaks that have been displayed in sideshows over the past 150 years, the Ubangis, remains the number one attraction of all time.

A Frenchman, Dr. Ludwig Bergonnier, first became aware of these big-lipped women at a Paris exposition of colonial possessions in 1928. Doctor Bergonnier went to Africa and traveled 160 miles on horseback into the interior of the French Congo where he persuaded an old chief named Neard that taking his family on a world tour would make him the wealthiest chieftain in the Congo. For the next two years, Dr. Bergonnier displayed his band of freaks throughout Europe and South America. These natives of the Congo jungle were distinguished from other Africans by the practice of beautifying their many wives with grotesque enlargement of their lips. This disfigurement was accomplished by inserting wooden disks in the slit lips of girl babies, and increasing the size of the disks as the child grew. The larger the saucer, the more beautiful the woman. Some of these women had lips the size of an average dinner plate. This, of course, was long before the discovery of Botox for enlarging women's lips and breasts.

When John Ringling came across this group, he hired them on the spot for 1500 dollars a week. Of this amount, Dr. Bergonnier kept all but a pittance, letting the Ubangies make what they could by selling souvenir postcards.

So in the spring of 1930, the Ubangis debuted at the Bronx Coliseum in New York City. There were a few major problems. These people, 13 women and the chief, Neard, were from the jungles of Africa. They didn't use toilets, or showers, they ate only raw food, two meals a day consisting of oranges, bananas and raw fish—no plates, no utensils. But the biggest problem involved clothes and they insisted on appearing naked from the waist up claiming it was too hot. Eventually they were persuaded to don a shawl but this was often discarded during their appearances. The fact that the poor souls were half-naked made them more popular than their grotesque saucer lips. Everywhere the circus traveled, the Ubangis had to have their own accommodations since no one could stand to be around them with their custom of ignoring the use of anything associated with a bathroom, including toilets and showers. On the circus lot they were confined to a separate tent and on the road a special Pullman car. These people were natives right out of the jungle with a 130-word language. They remained with Ringling Bros. for two years during which not a single one of the group ever took a bath or even washed their face and hands. During these two complete eight-month seasons, the Ubangis were the stars of the circus. They did nothing but appear in the Big Top opening "march around" spectacle and sell souvenir postcards in the sideshow—and eat and sleep—18 to 20 hours a day. Even though they were straight from the jungle and totally uneducated, they quickly caught on to a few things. One was knowing that taking their clothes off attracted a lot of attention. So, anytime they were upset about something, off came the clothes and it didn't matter where they were at the time. The press loved it, and John Ringling was horrified the whole time he was counting the money from the best years the circus had ever experienced.

Another practice the Ubangis developed involved the selling of their souvenir postcards. Somehow, it did not take them very long to grasp the value of money. Although the postcards sold for a nickel, anyone giving them a dime or a quarter received only a mute, dumb stare and no change.

But the public was absolutely fascinated by them, they seemed to have an hypnotic hold on people. Men and women would enter the sideshow and just stand and stare at them for five or ten minutes, and then return for the next performance and stand and gaze at them again.

After two years with Ringling's and the previous two in France and South America, the 13 women began to get homesick and miss their 64 children back in the Congo. John Ringling had made an absolute fortune exhibiting these unfortunate people from one end of this country to the other. Their exploiter, Dr. Bergonnier, had died in Sarasota of a strange insect bite. The Ubangis had hated him for over a year and were constantly preparing doll-like effigie images and sticking pins in them and putting small string nooses around the neck. They were totally pleased with his death and felt it was a reward for the hexes they had placed on him. The women were not totally convinced of his death until they arrived back in Sarasota and viewed the body.

By this time Neard, the chieftain, had amassed quite a bit

53

of money, which he kept in a huge steel chest, double locked and always within his eyesight. The women were getting smarter and more restless and it was time to go home. John Ringling hired a boat to take them back to Africa, where, according to several sources, the chief bought a sizeable ranch stocked with cattle and lived with his wives, the good life for the rest of his days.

Ringling Brothers followed the Ubangi act with another famous exhibition of ritually disfigured women. The "Giraffe-Neck Women of Burma," these people demonstrated the stunning results of their cultural practice of gradually elongating their necks with heavy, solid brass, coils. Once again, in their native surroundings, the elongated necks were considered a mark of beauty, the longer the better. The girls' mothers had slowly stretched their necks beginning in early childhood and adding coils each year until each girl's neck was approximately 16 inches long. These women also wore brass coils around their wrists and legs, the total weight of all these rings was between 50 and 60 pounds.

The "Giraffe-Neck Women of Burma" or "long-neckers" as the co-workers called them, never provoked the curiosity and popularity associated with the Ubangis and their saucer-sized lips.

There were certain sideshow features that were always present: the sword swallower, the fire-eater, the rubber man, snake charmer and the fat lady. Dolly Dimples, born Celesta Herrmann in Cincinnati, Ohio, in 1901, became the most famous fat lady for the circus. Strangely, Dolly's fame was not due to being fat, there have been a lot of circus fat ladies that weighed more than Dolly, her fame came from just the opposite. As a baby, she was of normal size, even as a toddler she was considered average; but when she entered grade school, she became fascinated with food. By the sixth grade, Dolly weighed 150 pounds and she never finished high school due to the harassment and bullying of fellow students. When she dropped out of school, she weighed 300 pounds.

Then she met Frank Geyer, who was slim and trim at 135 pounds, but he loved large ladies and encouraged Celesta to gain even more weight. She gained over one-hundred pounds in one year and the couple was married. While on vacation in Detroit, a carnival owner spotted the couple and hired her on the spot. Celesta took the name Dolly Dimples and was billed as the "World's Most Beautiful Fat Lady."

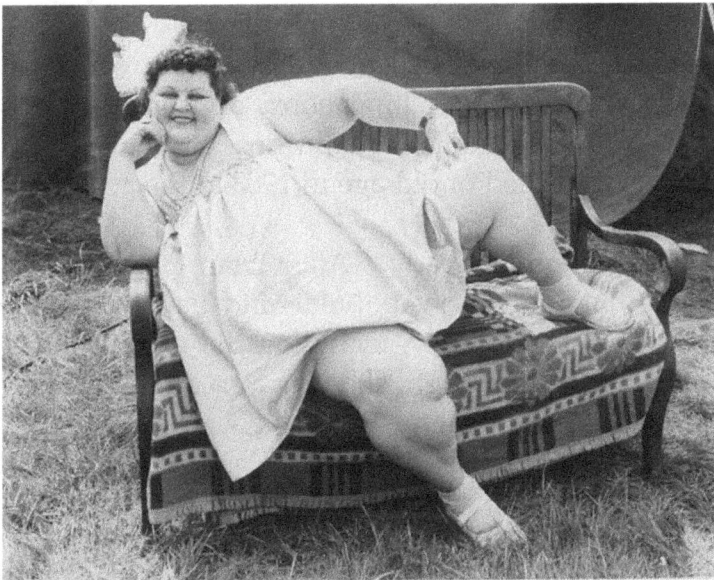

Dolly Dimples weighed 555 pounds and toured as the circus fat lady for 20 years. Faced with a severe medical risk she lost 443 pounds in one year, a Guinness Book record.

All her friends, including her husband, encouraged her to become even larger so she would be an even bigger attraction.

By the time, she began touring with Ringling Bros. she was four-feet, 11-inches tall and weighed 550 pounds. Dolly toured as the circus fat lady for almost 20 years. Then, in 1950, she had a nearly fatal heart attack. Doctors told her that it was a close call and she would have to alter her diet of 10,000 calories per day and lose weight or die.

Dolly Dimples loved life and she reacted to the doctor's advice in a most astounding fashion. In 14 months Dolly lost over 443 pounds, she went from 555 pounds to a svelte, petite 112 pounds. How did she do it? By eating only baby food! Dolly entered the Guinness Book of Records for the largest weight loss in the shortest period of time.

At the age of 50, Dolly entered a new career as a diet expert. She wrote a best-selling book, appropriately named "Diet or Die: Dolly Dimples Weight Loss Plan". She also ran an art gallery and died of old age in 1983 at the age of eighty-two.

Another famous fat lady, "Alice from Dallas", was not only heavy but immensely popular and had many famous friends around the Country, including the prize fighter Jack Dempsey. Strangely enough, she was also a big buddy of all the midgets. Can you imagine that?

Alice toured as the Ringling Bros. "Fat Lady" for 20 years. She was one of the very largest fat lady attractions weighing 685 pounds with a six-foot waist at her peak.

Alice, who was married, retired from the circus, lost 200 pounds and fittingly moved to Dallas, where she passed away at the age of 62.

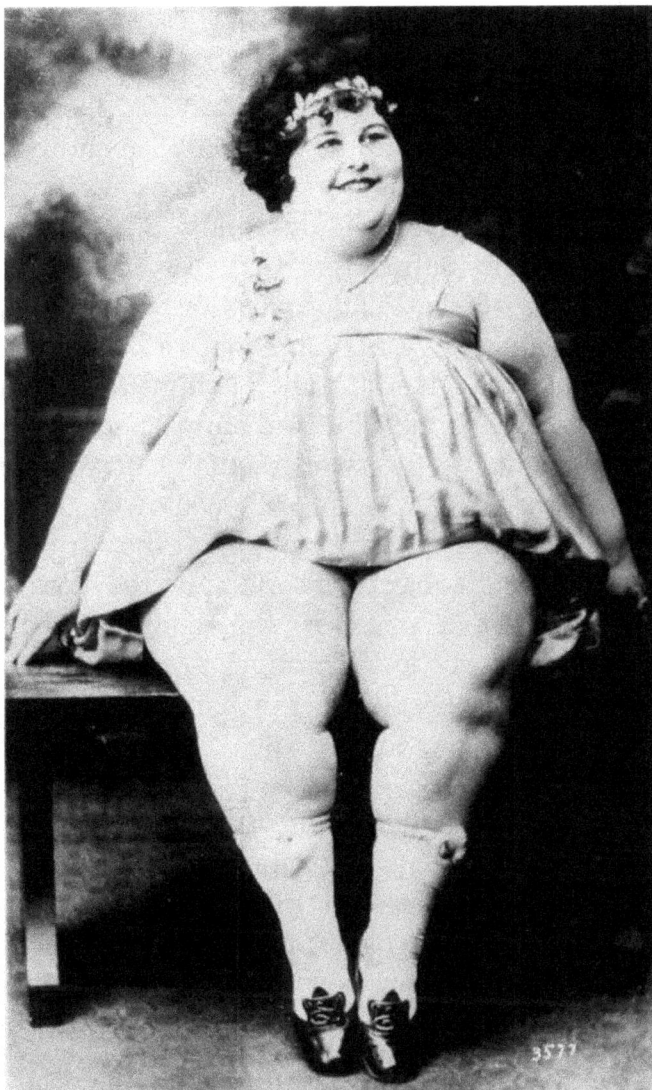

"Alice From Dallas" weighed 685 pounds and toured with her husband for over 20 years. She lost 200 pounds and fittingly retired to Dallas, Texas.

A sword swallower has to have a well-studied knowledge of the human anatomy. When the face is tilted backward at the proper angle, the throat and the esophagus tube make a straight line to the stomach. Depending upon a person's height, this tube is from 12 to 18 inches long. Sword swallowing, as an attraction, surprisingly dates back several thousand years and is first recorded to have been done at festivals in India. Today, many viewers believe that sword swallowing involves some sort of magic trick or illusion, such as a retractable blade, and some demonstrations may be performed in that manner, but the stunts performed in the major circuses involve the sword actually being swallowed by the performer. For the sword swallower the greatest obstacle to overcome is to learn to conquer the normal instinct to gag when a foreign object is inserted into the throat.

The Guinness Record for the length of a sword swallowed is 22.8 inches. Through the years, numerous performers have enhanced the act by using multiple blades at one time, or an actual Army-issued bayonet, and even a blade from a carpenter's saw.

The fire-eater is another staple of the sideshow attractions and this stunt is still being performed around the world. Usually the fire-eater coats his mouth with a form of non-flammable grease or just plenty of saliva. He then thrusts a kerosene soaked flaming torch into his mouth tightly compresses his cheeks and blows outward against his cheeks so the fire does not enter his lungs and nasal passages. After a second or two, the still burning torch is pulled out of the mouth with a great cloud of smoke and flame. If the performer wishes to extinguish the flame, the torch is left in the mouth a few seconds longer and lack of oxygen extinguishes the fire.

Fire breathing is a sister act for the fire-eater and involves filling the mouth with a flammable liquid, lighter fluid for example, and blowing the liquid thru a flame or torch. This is an extremely dangerous stunt and is currently performed by members of several rock bands, most notably KISS.

The basic sideshow acts have always included these essential elements:

- Freaks---human oddities like the Siamese Twins.
- Anatomical wonders---Hercules, contortionists, the fat lady, the "rubber man".
- Created oddities---tattooed lady, body piercing
- Working acts---fire eater, sword swallowers, knife throwers, walking on hot coals or sharp spikes.
- Illusionists---magic acts, saw the person in half, rabbit out of a hat.
- Animal shows---three-legged cow, two-headed goose, educated horse.

This type of entertainment, probably fortunately, has pretty much totally disappeared from the American circus. Some traveling carnivals and specialty shows still include a few of the sideshow acts, mainly limited to forms of magic and acts of unbelievable skill. For the American public seeing a fat lady, a seven foot giant or a tattooed body is not a big deal anymore.

Goliath was an elephant seal that weighed 7,000 pounds and was over 16 feet long. His tank occupied one-half of a 70-foot railcar.

THE MENAGERIE

The menagerie tent was big, larger than the sideshow tent and connected directly to the Big Top so the performing animals could enter and exit for their various acts. A ticket to the Big Top entitled you to enter the menagerie tent which opened around 11:30 a.m., more than an hour before the big show. As soon as you entered the tent, you could hear the big band, all 36 pieces, playing circus music---happy, rousing, fast and loud. My father was in heaven, he just was fascinated by unusual and exotic animals. The circus spent most of its time in small towns like Olean, towns without a zoo. Many week-ends my family would drive to Buffalo, a two hour drive each way, just to visit the zoo. Here in the Ringling menagerie tent was a wonderful collection of the more famous animals; lions, tigers, horses, and camels; but there was also a large array of unusual animals. These included 16 camels, an assortment of giraffes, including a baby, two rhinos, a mammoth sea lion and many others. The Buffalo zoo had two elephants while Ringling Brothers had 50 female Asian pachyderms.

The 50 elephants were cared for by 57 men who had no other duties. These men fed, groomed, and transported the elephants, but did not perform with them. If you cared to, you could pet the elephants, each one had a name, or give them some peanuts purchased from the "candy butchers" who seemed to be everywhere. The term "candy butcher" was another special term in the circus lingo that described the people who worked the concessions.

My father, being Irish, was especially attracted to the horses. Before the circus began to use trucks and tractors, Ringling's toured with a combined total of 750 performing horses and work horses. By the 1930's the workhorses had been replaced, but there remained a large number of riding and performing horses for the many equestrian acts, which were audience favorites.

Certain animals were special attractions, Gargantua, of course, was the biggest star, but Ringling had also acquired a huge walrus, two actually, that became a major attraction. They were sea elephants, (or elephant seals), the largest of the walrus family. These are gregarious animals named for their size and for the male's inflatable trunk-like snout.

When John Ringling found two of these creatures for sale at the Hamburg, Germany zoo he bought both to prevent a rival circus from acquiring the other and competing with him. One remained in Sarasota winter quarters and the other began appearing in 1928. For some reason the animal was a sensation from the opening show. Some attributed the phenomenon to America enjoying the period known as the "Roaring Twenties" when skirts went above the knee and weight watching became an important fad. It seemed a relief to stand and admire this Goliath "don't give a damn" approach to eating. Fifty or more fish were just an hors d'oeuvre to him and by the time he finished a typical meal several hundred pounds of herring heads, tails and bones, had passed down his throat. These southern elephant seals were typically about 16 feet in length and weighed around 7,000 pounds.

Goliath, the name Ringling's gave him, had to be in

water, of course, and his private tank occupied one-half of a 70-foot railcar. Each morning he had to be coaxed to wiggle his great body from the railroad car tank onto a flatbed wagon for the trip to the showgrounds. Once there, he had to slide into a portable canvas tank and wait his turn for show time. Goliath's "performance" in addition to appearing in the menagerie, consisted of riding around the Big Top track on a flatbed wagon.

After the evening performance, Goliath was returned to his tank on the train. During all these one-night stand transfers, Goliath moved albeit, slowly, under his own power. If he decided not to move the handlers' dangled fish in front of his nose, and slowly moved the fish in the desired direction, a great amount of patience was required. Some claimed it was more trouble transporting Goliath than getting one entire section of the train underway.

Eventually Goliath died, male elephant seals live to about age 14. The public was genuinely sad and demanded a replacement, and of course, Ringling had one ready.

As a measure of these creatures' enormous popularity, Dexter Fellows, long time Ringling press agent, claimed he received more requests from newspapermen for photographs of the two sea elephants than any other circus animal that inhabited the menagerie during his lengthy term with the Big One.

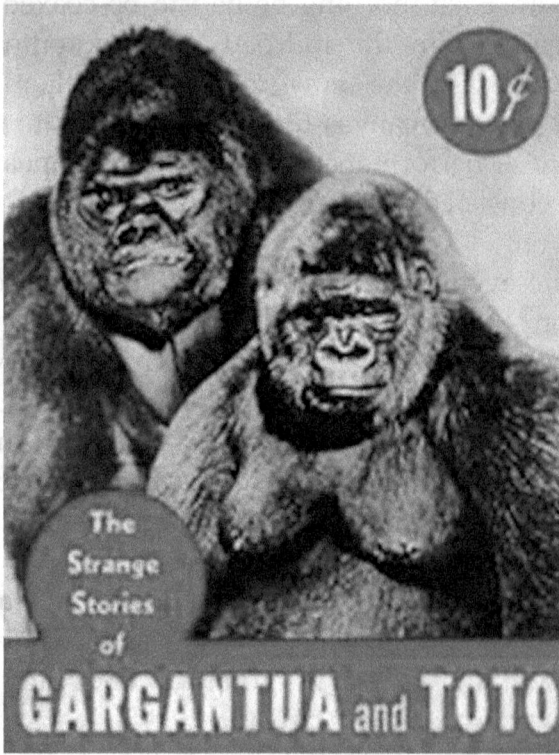

The gorilla, Gargantua, was promoted as the meanest animal alive. He was the main animal attraction for Ringling Brothers for 12 years. Gargantua weighed 600 pounds and had an arm spread of nine feet.

GARGANTUA

In all the history of the circus, there are two animals that achieved fame beyond all others. Jumbo the elephant will always be number one, but the other was a famous gorilla named Gargantua. For all his 11 years with Ringling Bros., he was the top attraction on posters and advertisements and especially in publicity.

The publicity apparently worked extremely well because my circus-loving father told stories for years about Gargantua and his super human feats of strength. In truth, he was probably the most dangerous animal ever kept in captivity. For all eleven years with the circus, no one ever entered his cage. The cage was divided into two compartments so he could be shifted from one to the other for cleaning purposes. The keepers, and there were eight of them, found the best way to get him to move was to borrow a snake from the snake charmer lady and wave it in front of the cage. All gorillas are afraid of snakes and it appeared snakes were the only thing "Gargy," as the circus people called him, was afraid of, and it worked every time. By the way, this was no ordinary cage. The cage, 26 feet long and 8 feet wide, was air conditioned and kept at a constant temperature of 76 degrees and 50% humidity. All sorts of furnishings were tried-- couches, mattresses, a chair swing, trapeze---Gargy just smashed them all to pieces. Finally, he was left with an automotive tire, which he could stretch like a rubberband,

and a chain trapeze. He was given a blanket every night and every morning it was torn to shreds. eleven years of a new blanket each day adds up to over 4,000 blankets.

Gargantua's life story is interesting, if not tragic. He was captured in the jungles of the Camaroons in central Africa when he was about a month old. At the age of one year, he was sold to an animal dealer and put on a ship to New York. Somehow, no one ever found out who or why, someone threw a bottle full of nitric acid in the gorilla's face. This terrible, senseless, and cruel act left the young gorilla with deep burn scars, and a twisted mouth that resulted in a permanent snarl. This incident may be what left the animal with a lifelong hatred of humans. Since the disfigurement lowered his value as a zoo exhibit, the gorilla was sold at a low price to a woman in Brooklyn named Gertrude Linz, whose hobby was making pets of unusual animals. She let the animal live in the house and named him Buddy.

For the next five years Buddy was a tamed household pet, even wore shoes at times. However, by now Buddy weighed over 400 pounds and had unbelievable strength. This strength was brought to poor Mrs. Linz's attention one day when Buddy squeezed one of her pet cats to an absolute pulp. Buddy was then placed in a cage where he became mean and unpredictable. On numerous occasions, Buddy bit and mauled a special trainer Mrs. Linz had hired to teach the gorilla some manners and a few tricks. By now, Buddy was six years old and Gertrude Linz decided she had better sell him. John Ringling North was in the market for a gorilla and Ringling Bros. circus was in serious financial trouble resulting from the prolonged financial depression of the 30's. Buddy was sold for $10,000 and after a few days of brain-storming by the circus press department his name was changed to

Gargantua. Then the press boys went to work making Gargantua into the "most feared animal on earth, the biggest, meanest gorilla that ever existed. The most terrifying animal the world has ever seen."

A lot of this was true. Gargantua now weighed about 650 pounds, was five-foot-five inches tall, and had an arm spread of nine feet. The snarl on his face and his frequent violent tantrums left no one denying that he was indeed a ferocious wild animal, and the Ringling press corps seized every opportunity to spread the word far and wide. Not long after Gargy arrived in Sarasota, John Ringling North, owner and president of the circus, furnished the press corps with a true piece of hot copy. North was explaining to a large group of visiting reporters how a day or so before, Gargy had reached thru the bars of his cage, nabbed a passing roustabout by the arm, pulled him against the side of the cage, nearly choked him to death and severely lacerated his shoulder. Unfortunately, North came just a little too close to the cage in his attempt to describe the incident from the day before, and Gargy grabbed him by the coat sleeve and began to chew on his arm. It took three of Gargy's handlers to rescue the president of the circus who spent several days in the Sarasota hospital. The story became "page one" in every newspaper in the country and around the world. Now everyone wanted to see this terrible animal.

Gargantua was quite smart and could be very clever. He loved to play catch with a softball, but he would always begin to toss the ball shorter and shorter distances attempting to lure you closer to the cage. He also loved tug-of-war, but once again he would make sure the rope became shorter and shorter and came closer and closer to the bars. Don't forget the nine- foot arm span.

In 1941, a great opportunity crossed North's path. A wealthy sportswoman, Mrs. Kenneth Hoyt, had caught a baby female gorilla while on an African safari in 1930. Just as Mrs. Linz had done with Gargy, Mrs. Hoyt had raised the gorilla, named Toto, in her home as a house pet. She even employed a keeper to care for the animal; but, once again, the gorilla became too big to handle and had a bad habit of biting people. North bought the animal and with much ballyhoo in the press announced to the world that Gargy and Toto would be wed at the Sarasota winter circus quarters before invited members of the press corps. Toto's air conditioned, double compartment cage was identical to Gargantua's. The cage was painted white for the occasion and a special wedding cake accompanied by Mrs. Hoyt was flown in from New York City. When the couple was pushed together and the bars raised, Gargy was absolutely stunned, but not for long. The very first thing he did was smash Toto in the face with a large cabbage and bite her on the arm. The bride responded by firing everything she could find at Gargy's head; she pelted him with oranges, grapefruit, cabbages, etc. Gargy went into one of his super rages, roaring and yelling and attempting to tear the bars out of the cage. The audience reaction ranged from hysterical laughter to absolute terror. The two eventually separated on their own, the bars were put down, and they lived separately ever after. Some circus folks accused the meanest, strongest, most terrifying animal in the world of being gay. After a few years, two baby gorillas were added to the display to keep the attraction popular.

Later that year, Mrs. Hoyt, Toto's previous owner, paid a highly publicized visit to see her old pet when the circus opened in New York City. Unfortunately, as had happened on too many occasions, Mrs. Hoyt got too close to

Gargantua's cage. He grabbed the back of her dress and Mrs. Hoyt was left standing in the middle of Madison Square Garden in her bra and panties.

Both gorillas ate about 20 pounds each day of raw vegetables, fruit, eggs, milk along with a small serving of meat. Gargantua consumed about a half dozen chocolate bars for dessert and Toto had red rose petals. Gargantua died of a lung ailment in 1949 at the age of 21.

In her later years, Toto became a television fan and a TV set was placed outside her cage just beyond her reach. She died in 1968 at the ripe old age of 38.

Gargantua was raised as a pet by a woman in Brooklyn. For the 12 years he travelled with Ringling Brothers, no one was able to enter his cage.

In 1966, Lou Jacobs had the distinction of being the first living American to have his image on a U.S. postage stamp.

CLOWNS

The big top was connected directly to the menagerie tent, which closed as a public entrance once the show began so the animals could enter and exit the arena.

As my dad and I entered the enormous tent, the size of one and a half football fields, the first thing that hit us, as a total surprise, was a circus clown. He arrived in the typical outlandish clown costume: red wig, big red nose, white face, red polka dot pajama-like suit, and floppy shoes. Well, directly in front of us, this clown tripped over his own big shoes, executes a perfect backward somersault, and simultaneously opens a big umbrella. Without a word, he moves on down the track and we are left laughing and trying to locate our seats.

As it turned out, Ringling Bros. had 60 clowns, each with his own individual costume and repertoire of funny acts. Clowns as a group have some common characteristics. One is they are irrepressible; it's built into the genes or somewhere in the makeup of every clown. They can't help it, they can't stop. If they're not on stage entertaining and fooling the public, they are playing practical jokes on each other or even better, on any poor sucker who happens to be unaware and available. Everyone on the circus knows, "steer clear of the clowns unless you want to be publicly humiliated." This is the reason Ringling Bros., provides them with private dressing quarters, known as clown alley, separate sleeping quarters on the train and totally separate dining area in the dining tent. These people are true satirists, pure caricaturists, and genuine artists. Beginning with P.T. Barnum and echoed down through the ages, it has often been said that to be a real circus you must have three things: elephants, acrobats, and clowns. Clowns remind you of a circus. What we must first understand is that to be funny, you have to be smart and clever, and clowns are usually talented in many lines. Examining the history of just a few of the most famous circus clowns reveals that each one of them was a talented performer before he became a clown. Some were inventors, musicians, dancers, bareback riders, tightrope walkers, jugglers, contortionists, scholars, acrobats, and pantomimists. Most of them are well grounded in psychology and sociology, and understand the human psych very well.

Since there have been kings and their courts, there have been clowns and jesters to entertain them. Today, the essential qualities remain unchanged. The art of the clown is to win applause by conduct so eccentric that he is considered an idiot whose truths may therefore be laughed away.

Clowning is not only an ancient art form. It also has rigid rules and traditions. It has styles of dress, make-up, deportment, and manners. Within clown art, there are three separate characters. The Joey, also known as "Whiteface," the Auguste, or "Proper" clown, and the Charlie, or character clown.

The Whiteface derives from the classic Pierote, the white clown of French pantomime and harlequin, the mischievous intrigue of French and Italian light comedy and English pantomime. His clown face is all white with the features (eyebrows, nose, and mouth) painted on in black or red and other decorations, if wanted, in various colors. When the features are life-sized, the clown is considered a "neat Whiteface." When the features are larger than life-size, he is called, "a grotesque White face."

The Whiteface clown holds the highest status in the clown hierarchy and is the oldest of the three clown stereotypes. When Whiteface clowns perform with other clowns, they usually function as the straight man, top banana or the leader of the group. A notable example of a circus Whiteface clown is Felix Adler, who performed with Ringling's for many years.

Felix Adler was noted for incorporating a piglet into his act. With his animal trainer background, he also used dogs, roosters, and even mules to entertain under the "Big Top" for over 40 years.

The Character clown adopts an eccentric feature of some type, such as a butcher, a baker, a policeman, a housewife, or a hobo or a bum. Character clown faces make sport of mustaches, beards, whiskers, freckles, warts, large noses and ears, baldheads, strange haircuts, or facial features.

The most well-known Character clown is the tramp or hobo, and this has been the case for decades. The great W.C. Fields performed in vaudeville, in London in 1901, as a tramp juggler. Charlie Chaplin made the tramp character universally popular with his many silent comedies beginning in 1914 and continuing all the way to 1946: The Tramp, 1915: The Gold Rush, 1925: and Modern Times, 1936. This sentimental clown was "the little tramp" that all the world loved-a victim who was a poet and a dreamer, just a poor common man that everyone could relate to.

There are many famous character clowns of the hobo variety, in both film and the circus. Notable movie examples include Red Skelton, who began with the circus, Larry Fine, of the Three Stooges, and Chico Marx of the Marx Brothers.

The hobo or tramp clown was not very popular with the circus until "The Great Depression" hit America in the 1930's, then many Americans had an up-close and real association with the tramp. In Olean, New York, our home was about four blocks from the railyard where switch engines maneuvered freight cars to make up trains. It was a common sight to see one or more hobos going from one back door to another begging for a handout before returning to the railyard to ride the rails to "God knows where."

The Auguste, or Red clowns, are usually the recipients of the comic doings. The Augustes are the ones that get the pies in the face, squirted with water, lose their pants or accidentally sit in wet paint.

74

The base color for the Auguste makeup is red or flesh tone. The eyes and the mouth are circled in white and the features are highlighted in red or black. The costume consists of baggy pants accented with polka dots or broad stripes. They wear wide-collared shirts, big long neckties, colored wigs and oversized noses and shoes.

It's difficult to imagine that within these three forms, Whiteface, Auguste, and Character, all clowns work. You may think there are exceptions, and like to think of the hobo or tramp as a fourth category, but if you examine the fundamentals, there are only three distinct types of clowns.

In the circus, the clown's act is known as a "gag." Gags are the clowns scripted and rehearsed performances. They can take place in the circus ring, on the circular track, or in the seats with the audience. These gags may be done solo, with other clowns, or circus performers, or even with members of the audience. They all have a beginning, middle, and ending; finishing with a "blow-off." The "blow-off" or ending, has a popular repertoire including the confetti bucket, the pants drop, a blackout, or the always popular "all clowns exiting running."

A fellow by the name of Dan Rice deserves special mention as the first American clown to achieve the status of the star. Born in New York City, on January 23, 1823, Dan Rice had to be one of the most talented human beings who ever walked the face of this earth. In addition to being the first clown star, Dan Rice achieved fame as a jockey, a gambler, a strongman who would catch cannon balls on the back of his neck, animal trainer, songwriter, commentator, political humorist, actor, director, producer, and politician. He ran for Congress, the Senate, and President of the United States-dropping out of the race each time.

Dan Rice's touring shows were the biggest entertainment in the country. He is credited with changing the circus into what it is today by mixing animals, acrobats, and clowns. His first big circus act included a pig named Sybil who could do a host of tricks including telling time.

Dan Rice had a tremendous following in the press and was a personal favorite of Mark Twain and Walt Whitman, and his talking and singing clown act took America by storm. During the middle of the 19th century, Dan Rice was more well-known and popular as a household name than President Abraham Lincoln. He died February 22, 1900.

The most popular clown who ever appeared with an American circus was without a doubt Shivers Oakley, who, from 1900 to 1910, reached heights which no buffoon is permitted to attain today. A tall, lanky Scandinavian, Oakley was natty in civilian clothes with his checkered trousers, buff suede spats, two-or-three tone shoes, and a solitary diamond ring the size of a walnut. Oakley commanded a salary that was at least 20 times greater than even the best fellow clowns were receiving. He is especially noted for one act, a solo baseball game in which he played every position on both teams. No matter where the circus was playing, his act actually stopped the show. His argument with the umpire frequently actually caused cases of hysteria in the audience that required professional medical attention.

Silent motion pictures began to be the big entertainment fad and Charlie Chaplin replaced Oakley as America's superstar. When he tried to return to Ringling Bros. they offered him 75 dollars a week as a walk-around clown act. Stardom is a fleeting thing. This initial "come down" coupled with being rejected by young vaudeville actress named Viola Stoll, even though she was in jail at the time for stealing his late wife's jewelry, resulted in poor Slivers Oakley, who could make everyone laugh, committing suicide by gas asphyxiation in his room in New York City on March 8, 1916.

As circus tents became larger and larger, acts like Shivers Oakley became more and more scarce. It's difficult to conduct a solo act that requires a "connect" with the audience when the audience consists of 12,000 people.

During the early 20's, Charles and John Ringling were running Ringling Bros. Circus. Charlie handled the day-to-day duties and John took care of the strategy requirements. One of their rare disagreements concerned the role of the clowns. John maintained that the long build-up the solo clowns required to establish a rapport with the audience slowed the entire show and reduced the excitement that a three-ring circus was designed to produce. Charlie held his ground and emphatically declared that clowns were a required fundamental element of a circus, especially Ringling Bros. "Greatest Show on Earth."

When Charlie died in 1925, John's opinion prevailed and he immediately abolished long clown solos. Only clown production numbers could be used and these were usually five minutes or less and appeared in the center ring to focus attention during moments of scene changing required for major accts.

Two major clown acts filled this need and became two of the most popular acts of the entire production. One was a burning house routine, which included an actual full-fledged fire, and the other was a clown wedding. One year John, who was not all that big on clowns from the beginning, decided that he and the audience had grown weary of the wedding routine and he retired the number. Well, John Ringling may have been tired of the wedding but public indignation was so strong, the act had to be reinstated in the show through the season and lasted many more years. Fire regulations in most of the larger cities ended the burning house number even though there had never been one incident, but the potential was certainly present at every performance. By the time the circus entered the 1930's, most of the clown acts were relegated to the hippodrome track doing little production numbers by themselves, or in small groups and there was very little time in which to establish a skit that emotionally engaged the patrons.

The Auguste clown is easily the most popular of the three types. The word Auguste comes from the German slang for "idiot," and the circus audiences in Berlin frequently shouted, "Auguste" as an insult to the early clumsy circus performers.

Lou Jacobs (1903-1992) was an Auguste Clown who performed for 62 years with Ringling Bros., from 1925 to 1985. That is one long time to be touring the USA and meeting the requirements of entertaining people in one-night stands.

Jacobs was born in Bremen, Germany to parents who had a touring song and dance act. Early in life, young Ludwig demonstrated great skill at acrobatics, particularly as a contortionist.

The family came to America in 1923 and Ludwig changed his name to Lou. He teamed up with another contortionist as a comedy act, and got a job with Ringling Bros. Lou Jacobs was in great clown company at the time since two other Hall of Fame clowns were also performing with Ringling's, Felix Adler and Otto Griebling and a little later, the great Emmet Kelly. Lou Jacobs is credited with numerous well-known circus clown acts, but the most famous one is the midget automobile, which occupied Ringling's coveted center ring for 20 years.

Lou Jacobs and his midget auto occupied Ringling's center ring for many years.

The act opens with the honking of an automobile horn and a tiny car races at high speed into the center ring. Visualize this and the car is continuously backfiring. It stops at a gas station in center ring run by a midget. One shoe almost the size of the car emerges, followed very slowly by the six-foot one-inch Jacobs dressed in the loudest imaginable plaid suit, red rubber-ball nose, a black mouth painted high in a white zinc grin, a 30-inch high celluloid collar with a bright red tie, a red mop wig and the biggest, floppiest shoes in clowning. The midget gas station attendant begins scolding Jacobs for parking too far from the gas pump. Jacobs whacks the midget on the head with a mallet leaving a balloon-sized welt on the midget's baldhead. Jacobs removes the radiator cap and a large snake jumps out followed by a geyser of water. Jacobs sits on the radiator to stop the water and it comes out of the top of his head, he attempts to stop this and the water spouts out of his mouth. Finally, the car is pushed to the gas pump. The midget then climbs into the gas pump and Jacobs throws a bomb into the pump. The huge explosion propels a dummy, an exact replica of the midget to the very top of the tent where a parachute opens and he begins to float back down. Jacobs climbs back into the tiny car and once again speeds out of the arena pursued by a policeman. This stunt took four years to perfect. As a contortionist, he was able to construct several tiny cars into which he was able to cram his six-foot-one frame, but none that would run. George Wallenda, a close friend and high-wire performer, suggested using a washing machine motor. Wallenda and Jacobs tinkered around for over a year making cardboard mock-ups that were smaller and smaller. Finally, they built a prototype and Jacobs got his fully dressed contorted clown body in and took it for a spin around the block in Sarasota, Florida, winter home of the circus. Unfortunately, because of Jacobs' huge floppy shoes, his visibility was compromised and he ended up by wrapping the tiny car around a large tree. Still, not discouraged, Jacobs and Wallenda built two more versions and both wound up stalled on the hippodrome track and pushed out of the tent in disgrace. Finally, in 1947, Jacobs had a model that was ready for the big time. The circus opened in

New York and Jacobs raced around the track at high speed; but once again a new pair of shoes obscured his vision and he actually ran over the policeman in the act, fellow clown Jimmy Armstrong. The collision broke the steering arm and Jacobs collided with a stage, wrecking the car. He had to be towed from the arena and hacksawed out of the car.

Another full year passed before the act was attempted again, and this time it was successful and went on for over 25 years. Jimmy Armstrong became the permanent policeman in the act and another famous Ringling clown, Frankie Sedisda, a midget, became the gas station attendant.

In addition to his famous car act, Jacobs made five other solo appearances at every Ringling performance for 25 years. The first of the five appearances featured two dachshunds on a leash. Each dog is eight feet long. Next, he comes on in another of his specialties where he is a one-man band. The drum, with a set of symbols on top, is strapped to his back and is played by a mallet attached to his ankle by a rope. Bells hang from a band around his head, and he is playing, quite well, a harmonica. This is followed by a stroll around the track smoking a six-foot-long cigar. We're not finished, and remember he did this on the road, twice a day for 25 years. Next, he changes to a formal costume, a red satin dress, and ostrich-plumed hat, carrying a birdcage containing an old shoe, which sings like a canary. Finally, he enters as a sheriff in a Wild West skit, shooting a loud pistol that caused a dummy to fly a hundred feet along the track.

It is difficult to imagine the large number of props, gadgets, and costumes employed in Jacob's routine. It took at least a half-hour for Lou Jacobs to paint his face, don his trademark red bubble nose, another of his inventions, and the rest of his costume, including the special shoes. And it took another half-hour to remove everything. He also had several other celebrated acts over the many years he performed, including a self-propelled bathtub and a skit where his pet Chihuahua, "Knucklehead" appeared as a mischievous rabbit.

In 1966, this incredible man, a German immigrant, had the distinction of being the first living American to have his image on a U.S. postage stamp. This was a man that arrived in New York City 43 years earlier with $2.00 and unable to speak English.

Jacobs was married to Jean Rockwell, a model, and circus aerialist. They had two daughters, one became a well-known acrobat, and trapeze artist, the other was an elephant trainer.

When Ringling Bros. decided the circus needed some fresh blood in Clown Alley, all the clowns were over 50, they established the Clown College in Sarasota, Florida in 1968. The school had limited success at first so they decided to add Lou Jacobs to the faculty. From then on the college was a total success. Not only was Jacobs a great clown, he was a superb teacher. Even when he retired in 1985, after 64 years of clowning, he continued teaching until he died peacefully in his sleep at age 89.

Otto Griebling was a tramp Character clown with the Hagenbeck circus when Emmett Kelly joined as a Whiteface. The next year they were both tramp clowns and together worked what was called a progressive clown stunt. Just before each show they would get a 25 pound block of ice, when the show began they would circle the hippodrome track with Emmett carrying the ice on his back and Otto calling up into the seats for " Missus Jones", who supposedly had ordered the ice. This would go on three or four times during the show, each time Otto is calling and searching for

Missus Jones and the block of ice is getting smaller and smaller. Finally, on the last trip, they spot Missus Jones and Emmett climbs all the way up and over the audience and delivers what is now an ice cube, and as he hands it to Missus Jones, it is only a little puddle of water in his hand.

The pair had a similar act in which Otto attempts to deliver a small plant to Missus Jones. He can't find her, and each trip around the track the plant gets larger and larger. Finally, the plant has grown to become a full-sized tree, which Otto delivers to someone in the middle of a row high up in the center of the seats. This was a typical clown act with Otto playing the Whiteface clown, even though dressed like a tramp, determined to get the job done while letting Emmett do the work as the Auguste clown carrying the ice or the tree.

In the mid-thirties, at the very height or depth of the Depression they created an act that generated vibrations across the entire country. It even acquired a name "the WPA Shovel Routine." Once again, Otto was the boss on the job and he had a roll of blueprints, stakes, and a measuring tape.

Emmett, wearing his trademark "Weary Willie" getup and carrying a shovel, was the worker. The boss is very busy measuring and pounding stakes to layout the plot of land. Kelly doesn't do anything but lean on the shovel, sit down and eat a sandwich, and look bored and tired. This, once again, is the classic White clown trying to get the Auguste clown to do something.

The Republican Party seized on a photo of Kelly leaning on a shovel as the vanguard for criticizing the whole Democrat/Roosevelt sponsored Federal Relief Program of the WPA (Works Program Administration), PWA (Public Works Administration) and the CWA (Civil Works Administration). The controversy grew to enormous proportions over what began as an innocent clown gag, and all the while, the circus enjoyed the publicity.

Otto Griebling began his circus career as a bareback horse rider and became a famous clown when an accident ended his riding act. Following his retirement Otto taught at the Ringling Clown School in Sarasota for many years.

Otto Griebling was born in Germany like his contemporary Lou Jacobs. It just so happened that the period prior to the First World War, 1914, Germany was the circus hotbed of Europe. This included many skilled artists: bareback riders, acrobats, animal trainers, and trapeze artists. Following the devastation of the war many, fortunately, emigrated to the United States.

Otto Griebling's father, a grocer, died when Otto was 13, and his mother emigrated to America leaving Otto and his older brother behind. Otto was apprenticed, for lack of any other opportunity, to a circus bareback rider. Under the European system apprentices received only training, food and lodging — no pay. After two years of this arrangement, Otto was unhappy; but he had become a very good bareback rider. In fact, years later he often substituted for star riders without the audience knowing or seeing any difference. Now, Otto's mother wrote that she was settled in Brooklyn as a boarding house operator and the two boys should join her if they could find their own passage to America. Emil, the older brother managed to secure passage by working on a freighter. For Otto this was not so easy. First, he had to escape from the apprenticeship where he had become a valuable piece of property and an income source for the manager. The plan was to run away in the port city of Bremerhaven, board a transatlantic liner as a mess boy, and leave the ship when it docked in New York. All went well until after two days at sea Otto found the ship was bound for Yokohama, Japan. So, it took nine months to reach New York. His mother located a job for him as an apprentice rider for Albert Hodgini, a famous English equestrian, whose act had been booked by Ringling Brothers. Otto and Hodgini did not get along from the beginning, and when the circus reached Madison,

Wisconsin the troupe missed lunch because of problems unloading the horses. Hodgini gave Otto five dollars to go to town and get some milk and bread for lunch. Otto went to town and just kept on going, eventually finding a job on a dairy farm where he worked two years. When Ringling Bros. returned to Madison two years later, Otto learned that Hodgini was still with the circus. He went to the grocery store, purchased the milk and bread, took them to Hodgini on the circus backlot, and gave him the change from the five-dollar bill. Hodgini was stunned for a moment, then smiled and said," It took you awhile. Get dressed for the act." He finished the season, then rode with the Tom Mix show, and eventually joined May Wirth, the greatest female rider of all time, where he performed a series of acrobatic clown stunts on horseback. In 1930, the act was a powerhouse, but ended when he fell breaking his wrist, leg and ankle; and permanently incapacitating himself for any form of equestrian act.

While recovering in the hospital, Otto Griebling decided to become a full-time clown, and he spent every waking moment improving his English, reading every type of book that might help him understand people better—books on psychology, books about famous actors and successful people, and critical studies of the art of acting and pantomime. Since his bareback riding and acrobat days were permanently over he learned to juggle while flat on his back and another stunt involving throwing a derby so that it went in a large circle and returned to him.

For the next 20 years, he toured with vaudeville shows, carnivals and circuses, but never with the "Big One". At last, in 1951, Griebling joined Ringling Brothers, "The Greatest Show on Earth."

Otto's acts required time to build an effect, so he preferred to appear in the "pre-show" when people were still entering the tent and the audience was assembling in their seats. One of these stunts involved Griebling in his clown outfit sitting on the edge of the circus ring knitting a sweater. Without saying a word, complete pantomime, he casually accosts a good-looking, well-endowed lady and asks her to try on the sweater for size. Whether the lady rejects his offer or agrees to try the sweater on, his pantomime act kicks into high gear of appreciation or disappointment. Another favorite stunt has him spotting an attractive woman with a male companion. He crowds himself between the couple, and when the woman turns to face him, his made-up face is only inches from hers, and his head is nodding up and down like he is agreeing with everything she is saying, even if she is saying nothing.

Once the show begins Otto has the run of the whole place, and he can be found anywhere and everywhere. He is dressed in the classic Charlie clown costume: black face with huge white lips, derby hat, and shirt without a collar, sagging trousers, torn overcoat, and large shoes. One moment he is in the center ring ready to catch an aerialist who is on a flying trapeze at the top of the tent. Next, he is standing behind a performer who has just completed his/her act, and Otto is graciously accepting the applause. Every once in a while he launches into one of his juggling or derby throwing tricks and becomes visibly upset when he feels he did not receive sufficient applause for what he considers the best act of the night. Otto also was frequently guilty of playing tricks on members of the show. One of his best involved the Ford Motor Co. who was a show sponsor. Ford was introducing their new line of cars in Cleveland and the Ford management was in attendance along with all the personnel from their ad agency. The event was rehearsed over and over again. The act involved the new Ford auto being driven to the circus center ring during intermission and popping out of the rumble seat would be Miss Cleveland, introduced by the Ringling ringmaster dressed in top hat and tails. However, when Fred Bradner, the Ringmaster, opened the rumble seat it was not Miss Cleveland. It was Otto Griebling and Emmett Kelly. The Ringling management, the Ford Management, the ringmaster, the agency personnel, all, well most of them, wet their pants. But the audience loved it and gave them a standing ovation. Despite this response from the audience, as you might expect from conservative corporate management, the act was not ever repeated.

Otto Griebling, spent 20 years with Ringling's. Even having his larynx removed following throat cancer did not stop him from performing his pantomime act and being an instructor at the Ringling Clown School. He was one of only four clowns designated Master Clown of Ringling's, the others being Lou Jacobs, Emmett Kelly and Frosty Little. Otto passed away in 1972.

Emmett Kelly, born in 1898 in Sedan, Kansas, was originally employed as a cartoonist. Kelly always wanted to join the circus and began practicing a trapeze act in his spare time. He was working as a trapeze artist with the John Robinson circus when he met and married Eva Moore, another trapeze performer, and they created an act known as the "Aerial Kelly's." You certainly would not want to have a serious argument with your spouse with this type of arrangement. He was the "leaper" and she was the "catcher." It was not until 1931, eight years later, that he created his famous character, "Weary Willie", a hobo he had sketched ten years earlier when he was working as a cartoonist. His routine was revolutionary at the time since all clowns traditionally wore whitefaces and bright clothes designed to make people laugh, and they performed silly slapstick stunts. "Weary Willy" was a sad, pitiful-looking guy, mimicking the many real-life hobos created by the Great Depression. There was even a weekly newspaper with nationwide circulation called the "Hobo News." His appeal to the audience was not for laughter, it was for sympathy and pity.

Kelly had two very famous solo stunts. The first was an attempt to crack a single peanut with a huge, over-sized sledgehammer. His most famous act involved cleaning up the circus ring with this tattered broom he usually carried. He began by sweeping up the edges of a single large spotlight. He was successful and the spotlight grew smaller and smaller; but typical of his pitiful character, no matter how hard he tried, he couldn't quite get that last speck of spotlight into his little dustpan.

He also had a stunt where he would spot an attractive lady way up in the bleachers. He would drag his pathetic body all the way up and as he got closer, his heart would begin to glow red, and soon it started to flash, and finally it was a red beacon. Kelly eventually became the most famous clown of all time. He performed with Ringling's from 1942-1955 and he was a major attraction. He took the 1956 season off and became the mascot for the Brooklyn Dodgers baseball team. In addition, he played his little tramp character in many movies and appeared on numerous TV shows. Emmett Kelly was a Master Clown and one of the first Clown Hall of Fame inductees.

Emmett Kelly created the famous character "Weary Willie," a hobo he had sketched earlier in life when he worked as a cartoonist. His son, Emmett Kelly, Jr., performed a similar act and became the most photographed and recognized clown in the world.

Kelly's son, Emmett Kelly, Jr., did a similar "Weary Willie" character and this, unfortunately, led them to be estranged for many years. Despite this family issue, Kelly Jr. became a very successful tramp clown. In 1964, Eastman Kodak Co. was looking for a suitable representative to appear at the company's Pavilion during the New York World's Fair. Kelly became one of the top attractions at the World's Fair two- year run. Kodak was so pleased with Kelly's performance at the highly successful Fair, they asked him to become their touring Ambassador of Goodwill. He was on tour for four years visiting thousands of towns and appearing at fairs, parades, schools, athletic events and hospitals. He easily became the most photographed and recognized clown in the world. Kelly, Jr. did not retire from clowning until his 81st birthday in 2004.

Felix Adler, born in 1895 in Clinton, Iowa, is another Hall of Fame clown and he was known as the "King of Clowns" when he performed with Ringling Bros. from 1914 to 1958. He was also known as the "White House Clown" due to his many appearances at the White House. He was a friend of three Presidents: Hoover, Roosevelt, and Truman. He was frequently photographed with the President's grandchildren and invited to their birthday parties. Felix Adler was also noted for his lifelong dedication to visiting children in hospitals. His hometown, Clinton, Iowa, honored him with the dedication of the "Felix Adler Discovery Center", children's museum, and each June the town celebrates "Felix Adler Days." Adler wanted to perform with the circus his whole life, and he did. He was expelled from high school because he concealed a live chicken in a teachers' muff. He ran away from home and joined a touring   league show, and then he joined Ringling's as an animal trainer. Adler was married in 1948 to another Ringling clown, Amelia Irvin.

Felix Adler developed a very distinctive appearance, which used two beach balls in a sling, like a brassiere, to pad his derriere. He carried a tiny red umbrella and had a large putty nose embellished with a birthstone, which he changed every month. With his animal trainer background, he was able to include dogs, roosters, and even mules in his act. But the one that became famous was a piglet named Amelia, after his wife. As soon as the little pig reached puberty he would visit a local farm and trade it for a new one, which he would begin to train immediately. He trained these little piglets to actually climb a ladder as he circled the hippodrome track.

And the piglet climbed the ladder ten times each time he completed a tour of the track.

The International Clown Hall of Fame and Research Center is located in Baraboo, Wisconsin, the hometown of the Ringling Brothers, and the original winter quarters of Ringling Bros. Circus. The center is dedicated to the preservation and advancement of clown art and achievement. It pays tribute to outstanding clown performances, conducts special events, and maintains a national archive of clown artifacts and history. The first inductees were elected in March, 1989; they were Red Skelton, Lou Jacobs, Emmett Kelly, Mark Anthony, Felix Adler, and Otto Griebling.

Red Skelton, born July 1913 in Vincennes, Indiana, was the son of a circus clown turned grocery store owner, and his mother was a cleaning woman. His career began at age ten when he became part of a traveling medicine show. He then spent time on a showboat, worked the burlesque circuit, and entered vaudeville in 1934. It was a pantomime sketch written by Skelton and his wife, Georgia, of how different people eat doughnuts called the "Doughnut Dunkers", which launched his career in vaudeville, radio and movies. His TV show debuted in 1951 and lasted 20 years. Once his TV career ended, Red Skelton concentrated on his artwork, particularly his painting of clowns. This hobby switched to a professional career in 1964, and it is estimated he made more money from his paintings than from his very successful TV show. He made over $2.5 million dollars a year on just lithograph sales.

Red Skelton always believed his life's work was to make people laugh and he wanted to be known as a clown because he defined it as being able to do everything. The Red Skelton Museum of American Comedy is at Vincennes University in Vincennes, Indiana.

Since 1989, some 61 additional clowns have been inducted into the Hall of Fame. These recent nominees have included Willard Scott, who played both Ronald McDonald and Bozo on TV before becoming well-known as the Today Show weather man, Max Patckin, the "Clown Prince of Baseball" and Meadowlark Lemon, the "Clown of Basketball".

The circus continues to change and Ringling Bros. no longer uses tents, and elephant acts are going to disappear this year, but that other circus mainstay, the clown, appears to be doing well. Clowns continue to be a part of the many smaller shows that are on tour each year. The two current Greatest Show on Earth touring shows have a dozen clowns.

Triple Self Portrait

Red Skelton was the son of a circus clown and his career began at age ten with a travelling medicine show. His TV show debuted in 1951 and lasted 20 years. Once his TV career ended, Skelton switched to his artwork, which was even more financially rewarding.

Fred Bradna, an Austrian, was the ringmaster or equestrian director of the Ringling Brothers Circus for 30 years. He could speak five languages and ran the circus like a Prussian drillmaster.

THE EQUESTRIAN DIRECTOR

The circus printed program with its wonderful colorful cover depicting elephants, clowns, tigers, trapeze artists and an enormous cannon contained a complete list and description of each of the 21 acts we were about to watch. As usual, the circus has a special term for each of these acts, they are called "displays."

At exactly two o'clock, right on the button, the curtain at the backdoor of the tent snapped open and in came the circus band in their bright red uniforms playing the loudest brassiest tune possible. The "Show" had begun with the traditional "Grand Entry," a glamourous parade into the "Big Top" and around the hippodrome that would set the tone for the rest of the afternoon. The band was followed by the rest of the performers, acrobats, ballet girls, and trapeze artists, most of them mounted on horses. Alongside were the exotic animals: zebras, giraffes, camels, even a hippopotamus. All this, of course, was punctuated by clowns eager to grab the show's attention with their sudden sight gags involving dogs, or pigs and skeletons. The end of the parade appeared just as the first part of the procession was beginning to exit the tent. The band stepped out of line and took their places on the bandstand where they continued to play until the "Grand March" was over. Bringing up the rear were the elephants, 60 of them, moving slowly, trunk to tail, and fashioned in their spangled blankets.

Now, the gentleman who was going to lead this show for the next few hours mounted his podium near the center ring. Known as the "Equestrian Director," not as you would expect, the "Ringmaster" who had his own job, strangely enough, in charge of the horse acts. The Equestrian Director title goes back hundreds of years to the beginning of the "modern" circus when horses were not featured acts but the very core of the circus, enabling it to travel from town to town and to do the majority of the work in assembling the tents and apparatus required each day. In the early 1900's, known as the "Golden Days" of the American circus, Ringling Bros. traveled with 750 horses. Just ponder the effort required to feed, water, groom, harness, and house and keep these animals healthy when the circus was on the road for eight months of the year.

The equestrian director was simply immaculate in his red coat, top silk hat, shiny black boots, and his all-important silver whistle. The equestrian director for Ringling Bros. was Fred Bradna and his rise to the loftiest position in the circus is an interesting tale. His "given name" was Frederick Ferber and he was born on May 28, 1871 in Strasbourg, Alsace, France, the son of a brewer-banker. Fred became a lieutenant in a crack cavalry regiment of the German Army. Ella Bradna was the star equestrienne with a small touring German circus. In the spring of 1901, Fred Ferber and a few fellow officers attended the circus where Ella Bradna was making her debut as the star act. In a true story, at the end of the act Ella's horse shied and actually threw her into the ringside box and the arms of Fred. In a fairy tale story, that was the beginning of a courtship that lasted a year, and ultimately a marriage that lasted 64 years.

Ella Bradna, also from Austria, was Fred's wife, and an equestrienne superstar. Her riding skills included a dazzling series of equestrienne acrobatics . It took one entire railcar just to transport her center ring act.

A year after Fred and Ella had their unusual introduction, Fred had resigned his Army commission and was backstage of the Hippodrome in Paris attempting to persuade Ellla to marry him. It just happened that a representative of Ringling Bros. named George Starr stopped by the dressing room and offered Ella a contract to join the American circus. Assuming Fred was her husband he included him in the contract as "Fred Bradna." Fred's job, according to the contract was to assist his wife. They were married the next day and Ella enjoyed 29 consecutive seasons of center ring stardom.

97

Meanwhile, Fred rose to equestrian director, where he stayed for 30 years and is considered "The Father of Modern Day Ringmasters." Once his name was on the Ringling contract as Fred Bradna, and he was getting paid, he decided to keep it that way and he was known as Fred Bradna for the rest of his life.

Bradna never lost his air of command and he ran the circus like a Prussian drillmaster. He was a perfectionist who would not tolerate the slightest letdown in any one performer or performance. Woe to the artist who thought he could get along with a slipshod performance.

Bradna could speak five languages and curse in several more. The equestrian director is the stage manager and master of ceremony of the circus---he is the "boss." He keeps the show on schedule so in two hours and 20 minutes it is finished. After all, this is only the matinee, the evening show will begin in just three hours and in between the 400 performers and 150 animals have to bathe and be fed. The director has to make sure the performers are on their toes insisting that each and every one give their very best. He has to adjust the show to meet urgencies caused by the weather, illnesses and temperament, (both human and animal), or malfunctions of rigging equipment.

The job of the equestrian director cannot be compared to a football coach or an orchestra conductor. Think about it, the equestrian director is managing 400 performers of varying types of skills, utilizing different rigging props and music, with many acts including dangerous wild animals. In addition, many of the acts are extremely dangerous, that's why they are in the circus. As a result, these performers are not your average next-door neighbor. They are tense, emotional, and definitely temperamental. This is to be expected from people who leap from a trapeze 70 feet in the air, enter a cage full of lions and tigers, or do standing backflips while riding horseback on a trotting horse.

A few more conditions help to complicate the director's job. First, is the fact the circus is constantly on the move. If you have ever moved your family you know it never goes perfectly, there are always some problems, the difficulty is you don't know what they are going to be — they are always unpleasant surprises---the water isn't turned on, the electricity doesn't work, the new neighbor won't let the moving van park near his house — endless surprises. Imagine moving 400 performers and hundreds of animals from town to town every day! In addition, since it is the director's duty to make sure each performer and act is executed at its very best, the director must be familiar with each of the acts or displays. This includes clowning, animal training, trapeze flyers, equestrians, tight wire artists, jugglers, etc. It's no surprise that Bradna would change his shirt six times during an average performance. He kept a box of shirts near the performer's entrance and changed during the clown acts.

While Fred Bradna was managing, leading and directing Ringling Bros., the girl that fell off her horse and landed in his lap at the Paris Hippodrome, the girl he married and he took her last name for his, Ella Bradna, had become the finest equestrienne in the world, occupying the center ring of the circus.

The original act that made Ella Bradna famous was a remarkable equestrian act with another outstanding performer, Fred Derrick. Derrick dressed in a tail coat and knee breeches for his act. It looked as though he was calling on the British Court of St. James. Ella wore a low-cut white bodice embroidered with sequins. Her long graceful legs were displayed in white tights. She had long white kid gloves and carried an ostrich-feather fan.

Ella entered the ring standing astride two galloping horses and lifting Derrick to her shoulders. From there she somersaulted to the ground and began an incredible number of leaps and pirouettes on and off the horse. Keep in mind the distance from the ground to the back of a stallion is over five and a half feet. Ella usually performed a few somersaults and leaps, and her specialty: a bareback toe-dance. The conclusion of the act revisited the two standing on the two stallions and performing a dazzling series of equestrian acrobatics in perfect unison.

As Ella aged the act was changed to accommodate the decline in Ella's skills. The display was known as "The Act Beautiful" and Ella made her entrance in a golden chariot pulled by a white-winged horse. A pack of dogs ran around and under the chassis while smaller ones tread milled on top of the wheels. A supporting cast of twelve showgirls and a bunch of pigeons dyed to match the girls' costumes completed the ensemble. It required an entire railcar to transport this one weird act, but John Ringling, a true sentimentalist remembered Ella's "glory days" and kept her in the center ring until she and her beloved Arabian stallion, "White Eagle" could no longer perform. It was an incredible effort, 29 consecutive years of performing breath-taking acrobatic stunts on the back of a galloping horse, all the while dressed like a queen and performing with unparalleled style and grace. Ella retired in 1942 and Fred retired in 1946. Both Ella and Fred Bradna died in Sarasota, Florida two years apart, Fred in 1955 and Ella in 1957. Both are enshrined in the Circus Hall of Fame.

THE CIRCUS BAND

My father and I had entered the Big Top around 1:30 for the matinee performance, which would begin at 2:00 o'clock. In the meantime there was a lot happening. First, we had to find our seats with 12,000 choices; but there were 60 uniformed ushers to help us. Most of the audience sat on bleachers, but for a little more money, you could occupy a chair, and for a lot more money you could occupy a cushioned chair near what would be the 50-yard line at a football game. At precisely 1:40 p.m., the 35-piece circus band under the direction of Merle Evans began to play and would continue pretty much non-stop for the next three hours. Merle Evans took over the Ringling Bros. bandstand in 1919 and continued as head bandmaster for the next 50 years. He was an absolute star at his profession. Born in Columbus, Kansas in 1891, he taught himself to play the coronet at age ten. At age, 15 he left home and joined Buffalo Bill's Wild West Show and toured the U.S. for the next 12 years. Once he joined Ringling Bros. it did not take very long until he was being hailed as the Toscanini of the Big Top. The all-brass circus ensemble played about 200 different pieces of music during a three-hour performance, twice each day. This was not an easy task since the music was keyed to each star's performance. The repertoire included a medley of fox trots, waltzes, gallops, marches, tangos and Latin numbers; along with Wagner,

Tchaikovsky and Sousa. The music had to have zip and expert timing, the worst thing that can happen to a circus act is a pause. Evan's credits include an illustrious career beyond the circus. He recorded and directed bands around the U.S. and in Europe, where his concerts included Bach, Beethoven, and Brahms. He was an outstanding coronet player, in addition to being a famous bandleader. He is also credited with writing eight circus marches.

Merle Evans conducted the 35-piece Ringling Brothers Big Top band for 50 years. Each performance, two per day, consisted of playing over 200 different pieces of music keyed to each star's act.

In addition to all these accomplishments, Merle Evans' quick reaction when the infamous Hartford fire broke out in the Ringling Big Top on July 6, 1944, is credited with saving thousands of people. As soon as he spotted the fire in the very top of the tent, he signaled the band to strike up John Philip Sousa's "Stars and Stripes Forever," the universal circus tune to signal an emergency. The performers heard the music and immediately began the rehearsed evacuation of the tents Accounts state that the band continued to play until the last moment, when it was no longer safe to do so. The band and Evans then performed outside and continued to play and help pace the evacuation and steady the crowd. The fire was the worst disaster in circus history, killing 168, with an additional 487 injured.

After his retirement at the age of 77, Evans continued a very active life giving workshops, and as a guest bandleader around the country. He died Dec. 31, 1987 in Sarasota, Florida, at the age of 96.

It is interesting to learn that Harry James, a famous trumpet player and bandleader from 1939 until his death in 1983, had his beginning with the circus.

Harry James' father, Everette James, was the director and featured trumpet player with "The Mighty Haig Circus." Mabel James, his mother, was a trapeze artist and continued to perform her aerial routines until a month before Harry was born on March 16, 1916.

Harry James traveled with the circus band for many years, learning the trumpet from his father. In addition, young Harry learned a contortionist act from one of the performers and they were featured together as, "The Oldest and Youngest Contortionists in the World." By the time Harry was nine years old, he was playing in his father's circus band, at ten he was playing solos, and at 12 he was leading one of the circus's two bands. Harry James progressed rapidly during the era of the big bands, 20 or more pieces, and several soloists, during the 1930's, 40's and early 50's. He was also well-known for appearing in several movies and marrying a famous movie star, Betty Grable. He died in Las Vegas in 1983 at age 67.

In addition to the band blaring, the clowns just about everywhere on the hippodrome track and in the stands, the crowd pouring into the tent and looking for seats, a fourth necessary ingredient added to the excitement: the concessionaires, or "candy butchers" as they have always been known in the circus and vaudeville world. These guys, commonly called just "butchers" sold peanuts, popcorn, crackerjacks, soft drinks, cotton candy as well as an array of novelties and official circus programs. They all worked on commission and some of them made careers of the job and had their own special nicknames: Pete the Tramp, Wacky Mac, Apple Annie, Good Looking Eddie, High Pockets, Camel Rider, Never Worry Murray, etc.. They were loud, aggressive, and good at their jobs. No one has ever been able to do anything but guess where the "butcher" title originated. These "butchers" often had to perform extra work just to obtain the privilege of operating their concession. In a small circus, the ticket sales pay the salaries and operating expenses — it is the concessions that provided the profit.

A quick review of the colorful program revealed there were going to be 23 "Major Displays" accompanied by countless sideshows, clown acts, and animal presentations. Now, this was a three- ring circus, plus two stages, so this entertainment is going to be going on simultaneously; they don't call it a "three- ring circus" for nothing.

THE FLYING WALLENDAS

The Flying Wallendas are most famous for their seven-person pyramid which is in the Guinness Book of Records as the greatest of all high-wire feats and has never been duplicated.

The first Karl Wallenda to be well-known in the U.S. was born in Magdabourg, Germany, in 1905, he was already the third generation of circus performers. By the time he was nine, he and his brother Herman were doing acrobatic feats in public, performing on the street and in restaurants where people threw money into a hat for tricks they liked. His high-wire career began in 1921 at the age of 16 when he performed a handstand on the shoulders of the famous aerialist Louis Weitzman, while Weitzman walked the wire. At 17, he and his brother rigged a bicycle with special rims to overlap the wire and he rode it between two church steeples 60 feet off the ground with Herman on his shoulders. At 18 he strung the wire across the Oder River at Breslow and bicycled across at a height of eight-five feet. By the time, Karl was 22. His brother weighed 185 pounds a bit of a load for a "topper" in circus parlance, when walking a wire 85 feet in the air without a net.

In Vienna, in 1927, Karl spotted an acrobat named Helen Kreis who had all the ingredients for his act. She was a fourth-generation trouper, with perfect poise and weighed 96 pounds. Helen had been working with her mother and sisters in a juggling and wirewalker act for four dollars a day. Helen joined Karl's act, learned to climb on his shoulders and keep her balance, and seven years later, they were married.

Another brother, Joseph, joined the act and they developed a high-wire pyramid act. Despite the originality and the daring, the act was not popular. Bookings were difficult to obtain mainly because many exhibitors were afraid of the act, fearing the Walendas would fall and result in all sorts of lawsuits, audience injuries, and bad publicity. In desperation, they accepted a booking in Havana, Cuba, and when the engagement was completed they did not have enough money to return home to Germany. They were actually sleeping in the park when fortune intervened. John Ringling happened to be visiting, heard about them; they performed an audition and he hired them on the spot.

The 1928 legendary Madison Square Garden opening night performance is considered the most exciting in the history of the circus. The excitement just grew beginning with the warm-up exercises, which seemed death-defying at a height of 70 feet, the very top of the arena. For the finale, Joseph and Herman rode bicycles in tandem across the wire with a pole braced across their shoulders. On the pole stood Karl and Helen. In the exact center of the arena, they came to a complete stop and Helen mounted to Karl's shoulders.

The crowd began to erupt even before the troupe reached the safety of their pedestal. Fred Bradna, the equestrian director, quotes in his book, "The Big Top," in a lifetime with the circus he never heard an ovation even half as loud. The crowd just could not stop yelling, screaming, crying and stomping their feet. The show was stopped for 15 minutes. Ironically the audience wanted the Wallendas to take a second bow. Meanwhile the family had taken only a cursory bow and rushed out of the tent to their dressing room. In Europe, whistling, shouting and stomping are expressions of derision. The Wallenda's unbelievably, thought they had failed; that all their hard work, including performing the extraordinary act without a net for the first time, had been received with contempt.

Fred Bradna had to leave his podium and go to the Wallenda dressing tent where he found the five of them sitting in total silence. They had already shed their costumes for street clothes. Bradna had to explain the situation to them, he was also German, and escort them back to the center ring where the cheering began all over again. This was the beginning of a love affair with the American public that continues to this very day.

The Wallendas seem to have some special ingredient in their genes that contributes to a rare combination of extraordinary balance skills with a calm, almost scientific approach to their performance. Unlike many, if not most performers, especially ones where their very lives are at risk each time they perform, the Wallendas are not superstitious or temperamental. They approach their twice-a-day act as a job to be accomplished by a dedicated team of professionals.

Consider the fact that a high-wire act performed in the controlled conditions of an arena where everything is identical night after night is a completely different situations than appearing in a tent. On a typical Midwest summer afternoon the temperature at the top of the Big Top could approach 100 degrees Fahrenheit, or there may be a severe storm with plenty of lightning, thunder and worst of all, wind. The complex rigging for the act is set up and torn down daily and since it is anchored into the earth, it makes a great difference whether or not rain has made the ground soggy. It was rain that almost wiped out the troupe in 1934. Once again, this outcome is close to unbelievable. First, when John Ringling was in charge he insisted the rigging for such a dangerous act be anchored into the ground by two telephone poles; but John had lost control of his circus. The rigging was now anchored by "dead men", blocks of concrete set on the ground. Things had gone well during the early afternoon warmup acts despite the fact rain had been falling all day. Just as Helen mounted to the shoulders of her new husband, Karl, one of the "dead men blocks" slipped about six inches. This much movement was enough to only make the wire go slack, but it was sufficient to upset the Wallendas delicate balance and the wire began to tremble violently causing the entire group to fall. Remember: 70 feet, seven stories, and no net.

Karl, 29 years old, and in the prime of his life, grabbed the wire with both hands as he fell and thrust his legs out and caught Helen's head in an ankle scissors hold as she tumbled past him. His grip was so tight that Helen lost consciousness from the pressure. Meanwhile, Herman had also grabbed the wire with both hands and Joseph had grabbed Herman's legs as he fell. Herman then proceeded hand over hand along the wire until he reached the platform with Joseph dangling from his legs. Karl was not able to accomplish this while holding Helen in an ankle scissors lock; so, he held on until they both dropped into a safety net that had been spread below them. Bradna blew his silver whistle for the next act, the band struck up a lively march, and unless you had seen the Wallendas perform previously you would never have known that a near fatal accident had occurred. Now, the best part! The Wallendas performed at the evening show as usual. The only injuries were Helen with a bandaged head and Herman with a cut on his throat from the wire. The next day a reporter for the Akron, Ohio newspaper stated in the paper that the Wallendas fell so gracefully they appeared to be flying. The article headline read, "The Flying Wallendas," and the name is still synonymous with the family today.

Karl was never satisfied with the high- wire act and each winter in Florida he would experiment with more daring stunts. It took him eight years to develop what is listed in the Guinness Book of World Records as the greatest of all high-wire feats. No other aerial troupe has ever been able to duplicate it.

The act involves four men linked together by two shoulder bars standing on a wire holding balancing poles. Above these four, two more men stood on the shoulder bars below. These two are linked by another shoulder bar. On this shoulder bar Helen Wallenda balances a white wooden chair and then climbs up and sits on it holding a balancing pole. To top the act off as a final gesture she stands on the seat of the chair still holding her balancing pole. All of this without a net.

On January 30, 1962 at the State Fair Coliseum in Detroit Michigan, Dieter Schepp, a young nephew of Karl's wife Helen, was making his first appearance as lead man of the pyramid. He cried out "I can't hold on anymore" and the pyramid collapsed. Three men fell 40 feet to the ground and the rear anchorman remained standing on the wire. Karl and his brother Herman fell from the second tier and grabbed the wire. The girl in the chair, Karl's niece Christina, was caught by Karl and he held on until a net was in place. Both Dieter Schepp and Richard Fanghan, husband of Karl's daughter Jenny, were killed. Karl's adopted son, Mario, who also fell 40 feet to the concrete floor, was left paralyzed from the waist down. Karl's injuries included a broken pelvis and a double hernia. True to their show business roots, the Wallendas put a show together and performed the next night. Never again did Karl's wife Helen watch him perform and the "seven pyramid" was removed from the act and was only done again on two subsequent occasions. The very next year, 1963, the Wallendas performed it once to show that life goes on and disaster does not have to end in defeat. Again, in 1977, Karl's grandchildren performed the act once for the filming of the movie, "The Great Wallendas."

Following the accident Karl seemed to bask in the fame it created and he branched out into even more daring stunts, particularly high wire walks known as "sky walks." At the age of 65, in 1970, he took a 1,000-foot walk across the gorge at Tallulah Falls, Georgia. It took him 17 minutes and he earned $10,000. He performed many of these long solo walks and frequently paused in the middle and stood on his head on the wire, supposedly to rest. He often said, "life is on the wire, the rest is just waiting." He performed more and more awesome stunts as he grew older, walking the wire blindfolded, walking 720 feet between the Eden Roc and Fontainebleau Hotels in Miami Beach on a pitch black, blustery January night. He admitted it was extremely dangerous, but claimed he had to do it because all America was watching.

In San Juan, Puerto Rico, on March 22, 1978, at the age of 73 he began a 750-foot walk on a wire 12 stories high, strung between the Flamboyan Hotel and the Condado Holiday Inn. The stunt was being performed to promote the Pan American Circus where he and his 17-year-old granddaughter were performing nightly on a wire that was 50 feet off the ground. Everything was still going very well for Karl and after being absent from Ringling Bros since 1946 he had just signed a contract to begin performing again in the 1978 season.

As he crossed the wire, with the granddaughter watching, a gust of wind set the wire vibrating. Some witnesses blamed the wind, others claimed the gust wasn't that strong, and blamed it on a faulty rigging. This time, at 73 years old, Karl was not able to grab the wire and he fell over 100 feet to his death.

Two years later a grandson, Enrico Wallenda returned to San Juan and successfully completed the walk that had taken his grandfather's life. And the dynasty continues today with both group and individual high-wire acts. Nik Wallenda, Karl's great grandson, born in 1979, walked the wire across Niagara Falls at night, with TV cameras watching the breathtaking event that was shown live on network television. One year later, he performed a similar walk across the Grand Canyon. The seventh generation Wallendas are now appearing in several venues around the world.

On October 10, 2015 Nik Wallenda's wife, mother of their three children, performed at the Charlotte Speedway -- hanging by her toes from a helicopter, 150 feet above the racetrack.

The Flying Wallendas continue to perform around the world. The family members span seven generations and have been performing for over 120 years. Recent tight wire stunts include crossing Niagara Falls and the Grand Canyon.

THE LION TRAINERS

There is a good reason "a three- ring circus" is often used as a synonym for complete mayhem or chaos. As soon as the Wallenda's completed their high wire, act swarms of workers entered the ring and began preparations for the next performance. This did not mean the circus came to a halt or even a slight pause.

The clowns were busy everywhere with their silly stunts and a host of animal acts appeared on the two stages. Educated animals have always been a staple of the circus repertoire and this one had an abundance. On one stage, two dogs were seated at a table playing dominoes, while on the other stage a group of four pigs intently played a game of blackjack. All these animals were appropriately dressed. Meanwhile, on the track, ponies walked on their hind legs carrying schoolbooks and a trained rat climbed a pole and raised the American flag.

All of a sudden, the lights dimmed and a spotlight illuminated the center ring and the music took on a more serious tone. While all the silly chaos had us distracted a huge cage had been erected and inside this cage on individually lighted pedestals were, once again, believe it or not, three polar bears, two black bears, eight Berber lions, two spotted leopards, two Bengal tigers, a black jaquar, two wolves, and two Great Dane dogs. These animals are wild and natural enemies, and here they were together in one big cage. It sort of took your breath away and for an instant the audience was completely silent. Then the applause and cheering began. Newspaper writers generally considered this the greatest wild-animal act of all time because, in addition to being together in the same cage, these animals were each going to perform their own unique act. Tigers leaped through rings of fire, even though they are naturally scared to death of flames, dogs rode on the backs of lions and polar bears, and black bears mounted their pedestals knowing exactly the one reserved for them. As the lights were turned up we noticed there were cages with wild animals in all three rings. Reviewing the history of Ringling Bros, it's surprising to learn that in the "Golden Days" of the circus, 1920's, John Ringling decided "The Greatest Show On Earth" did not need wild animals and he dropped animal trainer acts from the spectacle. He felt they were too dangerous, took up too much time erecting the cages, cost too much money in feeding, transporting, and medical bills and were a source of constant negative publicity from animal rights activists who claimed the training regimes were cruel. He had some pretty good reasons for the decision. When John lost control of the circus the new management returned wild animals to the show, and they did it with one of the most famous trainers in circus history---Clyde Beatty.

Clyde Beatty was born in 1903 in the small town of Bainbridge, Ohio, the oldest of nine children. As soon as he graduated from high school, joined by his friends, he ran away with a visiting circus. He began at the very bottom cleaning the cages of the wild animals but soon discovered that he had a special trait for getting along with the animals.

It did not take very long for Beatty to decide to strike out on his own with his special animal trainer act. Beatty entered the cage dressed like a big-game hunter in the African jungle; pith helmet, cavalry shirt and jodhpurs, and knee high black boots, carrying a big whip and chair and armed with a pistol containing blank cartridges. At times, his act would include 20 lions and 20 tigers in the same cage. The act proceeded at a rapid pace and the idea was to demonstrate Beatty's complete control of the wild beasts; there he was cracking the whip, firing the pistol and thrusting the chair in the face of the growling animals as they went through their trained paces of leaping from pedestal to pedestal, standing, etc.

The act was immensely popular and Clyde Beatty was already famous when he joined Ringling Brothers. He developed the act to the point it would appear he was actually fighting with the beasts. In 1932, at winter quarters, while rehearsing the act Beatty was severely bitten by Nero, one of the older lions. Infection was always the ultimate danger from a cat bite, and, sure enough, Beatty wound up near death. With no antibiotics available in 1932, penicillin was not discovered until 1940's, surgeons excised a chunk of Beatty's thigh all the way to the bone and saved his life. It took him 10 weeks to recover. Clyde Beatty was such an important part of the Ringling Bros. circus that the New York Madison Square Garden opening was delayed for his recovery and return to the show. Beatty and his "fighting wild animal act" became so popular that he eventually had his own circus, which later combined with the Cole Bros. Circus. In addition, Beatty appeared in major roles in six Hollywood movies and had his own syndicated radio show for several years.

Clyde Beatty and his "fighting wild animal act" became so popular that he had his own syndicated radio show, appeared in six Hollywood movies and even had his own touring circus.

Beatty married Harriet Evans, a young dancer from Russia, who joined the circus selling candy (a candy butcher) since she was out of work and desperate during the Great Depression of 1933. Beatty taught her the lion tamer techniques and she became quite famous and popular on her own as part of Beatty's show. They were together until her death from a heart attack in 1950. Beatty continued performing until his death from cancer in 1965 at the age of 62.

The lion tamer act my father and I were about to witness involved an entirely different approach than the Clyde Beatty show. When Beatty left Ringling's he was replaced by Terrill

Jacobs, and in 1940 by a Frenchman named Alfred Court. Alfred Court revolutionized the art of training wild beasts, and he is considered the greatest animal trainer of all time — and there have been many great ones.

Court was not pleased with trainers of what was known as the "Hackenbeck School", where the wild animals were "gentled" using blank pistols, chairs, sticks and whips. Court set out to prove that kindness, a soft voice and a lot of patience worked much faster and better than cruelty.

Alfred Court came from a wealthy, aristocratic family but he seemed to have the circus in his veins and ran away from home at age ten. He was returned by the police and settled down to become an accomplished acrobat and tumbler. The family eventually let Court organize his own small travelling show. One of the shows' major attractions was a four-lion act. One day the trainer was severely mangled, a somewhat common occurrence in those days, and rather than lose the act, Court took over without any previous experience. He loved it from that day forward, and the animals seemed to like him. Since he had no previous training or experience he made up his own methods as he went along, and the basis from the beginning was kindness. Nowadays, his techniques are used by all animal trainers.

If kindness were the cornerstone of Court's approach, patience was the key ingredient. Using lions as an example, like humans, they have different levels of intelligence and different dispositions. Only about one out of every five lions is intelligent enough to even begin training. Of the one in five that can be trained, most of these are able to learn only one or two tricks. But every once in a while along comes a cub that is just born for the show ring. This is the animal that is the "end of the rainbow" for every trainer.

117

In addition to the differences between lions, there are major differences among animals. The tiger is much more intelligent than the lion and, as a result, can be taught many more tricks such as walking a wire or jumping through a hoop. But as the tiger grows older he becomes meaner. The lion slows down, as he gets older and sort of gives up the fight and accepts the role in captivity.

What makes Court's act so special is understanding how difficult it is to train any wild animal and how each of them requires special techniques. The jaguar is smart and trains relatively easily, but when it's time to perform, he is very likely to refuse. The black panther is an impressive animal with tremendous speed and very good intelligence, which makes him easy to train. The problem is his reactions and speed are too quick and he is a killer. When you see a tamer in a cage with a black panther, you are seeing a brave person. The most difficult animal to train is the bear. We have all seen the bear riding a bike, standing on a ball, even roller skating. Teaching bears to perform these tricks is not only extremely difficult, but it is very dangerous.

The bear is a lot more likely to injure or kill you than a lion or tiger. First of all, thanks to Teddy Roosevelt and our famous teddy bears along with the wonderful photos of playful bear cubs, we tend to let our guard down when dealing with bears. This is the major reason for the unfortunate fatal and near fatal incidents involving bears and park tourists every year. The bear always looks the same, there is no warning of an attack. The lion roars, the tiger's ears will lay back, even the elephant will sway his trunk when unhappy. Not the bear, he is just deadpan, that big paw and claws just seem to come out of nowhere. Surprisingly the bear does not even have to draw back his paw before he strikes you.

One other physical trait that makes the bear especially dangerous is his teeth. They fit together like a piece of tongue and groove wood, and as a result, they cannot be pried apart. This is a gift of nature and evolution at work, and it enables the bear to catch and hold slippery fish. Unfortunately, once the jaws of the bear come together it will not let go. With a lion or tiger, you can scare it into releasing its jaws by firing a blank pistol or using a whip, even the elephant will quit if shown a small flame, but nothing will persuade the bear to stop. In addition, just like the claws and jaws of most animals, the bite is exceedingly toxic.

If a bear is going to become a performer in a circus, the training must begin before it is six months old. The basic method used to train a bear is the same as it is with all animals---demonstrate what you want them to do and reward them when they do it. And the reward is always the same—food. The food is not the same, of course, bears love berries, bananas, apples and lettuce; tigers and lions are carnivores, and the reward is meat. The difference in training the bear versus other performing animals involves the technique employed. Bears are trained in the opposite direction. The mentor finds out what skill the bear has and then encourages it to use it. You cannot train a bear to stand on its hind legs, no amount of coaxing, demonstrating or rewarding will teach him the trick. But if he stands on his hind legs naturally, then you can easily exploit this trait. You might be able to have the bear roller-skating in six months. The use of bears in acts has one more problem; if you decide to mix breeds, beware. The black bear, grizzly bear, polar bear, and the Himalayan bear are all natural enemies.

Now just consider Alfred Court's main act included three polar bears, two black bears, eight lions, two tigers, a jaguar, two wolves, and two Great Danes---all in the same cage!

Alfred Court and his wild animal act were extremely popular in Europe when John Ringling North decided to bring him to the United States to replace Terrill Jacobs who had been touring with Ringling's for two years with a three-ring, 17-minute act, featuring 50 lions and tigers. Court arrived with 80 animals, 50 tons of baggage and four trainers.

In addition to Court's gentle and patient approach to training animals, he also was absolutely meticulous in caring for them. As a result, when Court's wild animals entered the ring to perform they looked like a million dollars—alert, glossy coats and ready to perform. Feeding wild animals and keeping them healthy is extremely important and difficult. For example, Court would not allow one of the big cats to be fed if there was a speck of sawdust on the cage floor—it might get indigestion. All the cats, regardless of type, were fed once a day, usually about 16 pounds of horsemeat. Court varied this diet each week, on Sundays they received warm milk with eggs and a mix of vitamins.

Animal trainers, from Clyde Beatty and Alfred Court to the most fabulous female trainer, Mabel Stark, all report that it is a joy to work with members of the cat tribe. They say you can tell they actually enjoy performing when properly trained and healthy. The ring is a welcome change from the confinement of their cages. The act gives them a little freedom to leap, stretch, and do other exercises. And, of course, there are the little morsels of meat that come as a reward for performing.

When the show opened in New York City, Court had 60 animals working in three rings at the same time. Included were lions, tigers, black jaguars, snow leopards, black panthers, pumas, cougars, polar bears, Himalayan bears, mountain lions, spotted leopards, black leopards, spotted jaguars, ocelots, and Great Dane dogs. This was the greatest variety of wild animals ever presented at one time. The amazing part was that not only were these naturally wild animals mortal enemies of each other appearing in the same cage, they were performing an amazing variety of tricks. Newspaper writers described the show as breathtaking, and at times, the audience remained totally silent before bursting into applause. It was indeed the greatest wild animal act of all time, and lasted a full 20 minutes.

Alfred Court had assistants, but he was personally involved in training each of these animals, and they all knew him and appeared to respect and like him. For most of the shows, Court remained on the sidelines in a supervising role and let his assistants present the animals in the ring and accept the bows. One interesting sidelight: when Court finally retired in 1945 at age 62, he was the only animal trainer to leave the business without ever being seriously attacked. He was also the first to develop the trademark ending of the act by walking around the arena with a live leopard draped around his shoulders. This ending for the act resulted in a standing, cheering ovation every time, twice a day, for five years.

Alfred Court and his wife retired at age 62 to their villa near Nice, France, where he became a prolific writer and his memoirs have been published in several languages. Court died in 1977 at the age of 84 and is buried in Nice

Mabel Stark deserves to be mentioned when describing the best trainers of all time. She was born December 10th, 1889 in Tennessee. One of seven children, her given name was

Mary Haynei. By the age of 17, both parents had died and she and her siblings were orphans. After living with relatives and working as a nurse, she eventually found her way into the travelling circus and carnival business, as a dancer and horseback rider. In 1911, she met and married an animal trainer, Al Sands, and from then on, for the rest of her life, she was training, and taming wild animals. She was married at least five times, like Lillian Leitzel, the trapeze star she claimed she could not remember everyone. She probably could remember the number of times she was mauled, bitten, and clawed by big cats. In the space of three years, she suffered three major attacks. On February 18, 1916, Stark was severely mauled by a lion during a rehearsal with her husband, Louis Roth. The lion seized Stark's arm into its mouth and began rolling over and over. Roth was able to fire a series of blank cartridges into the animals face. Mabel Stark was dragged unconscious from the cage and rushed to the hospital where she was treated for a mangled and broken arm. Two years earlier she had been attacked by her leopards during a parade in Detroit, Michigan; and just the year before, 1915, she was mangled by a tiger in Venice, California.

Mabel Stark kept coming back for more and there were many, many additional incidents. The big break for what became her famous trademark act occurred when she adopted a mangy, sickly tiger cub named Rajah. She actually raised the wild animal in her apartment and would often take him to the beach to romp and play. The feature of her act when Rajah was fully-grown involved the tiger running straight toward her, rearing up, on his hind legs and wrapping his forefeet around her neck. Stark would playfully throw him to the ground and they would roll around three or four times before, she would put her face in the tiger's mouth, then jump to her feet and bow to the audience. The act was quite violent and the audience would think she was being mauled by the tiger when actually what was happening was just the opposite. It was at this time that Stark began wearing her trademark white jumpsuit to hide the tiger semen.

The animal trainer act was always featured in the center ring.

She joined Ringling Bros. in 1922 and performed with Rajah, 12 other tigers and a black panther. By the end of the season, of the six wild animal acts featured with the circus, Mabel Stark's act was number one and she became the center ring star. She claimed the top spot until 1925 when John Ringling decided to abolish all wild animal acts because "they were more trouble than they were worth." To complicate the situation it just so happened that Mabel was married to the Ringling Bros accountant at this time and he was found embezzling from the circus. Although the press release stated the reasons for ending the animal acts were because they were too dangerous, parents felt they frightened the children, the big steel cages took too long to set up and tear down and the animals were too expensive to feed and transport. Stark always felt John Ringling, an impetuous man for sure, was punishing her for being married to the embezzler. People who knew John Ringling well seemed to agree that the marriage may have at least played a part in the decision to end the wild animal acts.

At this time, she was the leading animal trainer in the world, male or female, and the center ring star of the circus. She had her own private railcar, which was right behind John Ringling's car on the circus train. Canceling her act was a big blow to absorb. In addition, she was still under contract to Ringling Bros, which stipulated that she make herself generally useful. The management placed her in a horse-riding act, which she had done 20 years earlier. Mabel Stark was just miserable without her tigers, but just at the bottom of her life, finally, she truly fell in love with a guy for the first time. To say the very least it was a strange situation.

Art Rooney was the manager of the menagerie and a strange personality at the time, 1920's. He never dated any women, wore finger nail polish at all times, and generally acted like a woman. But he really admired Stark at a time she really needed someone to admire her. The circus was absolutely stunned when they announced their plan to be married. Within two years, Art Rooney was dead and the cause remains a mystery to this day. There are several books written on the subject, including a very interesting novel, "The Final Confession of Mabel Stark" by Robert Hough.

Mabel Stark found work in Europe and returned to the U.S. in 1928 and travelled with the John Robinson Circus. In

Bangor, Maine, she slipped in a muddy arena and was seriously mauled by several tigers. One of the many wounds almost severed her leg and others tore a hole in her shoulder and severely lacerated her face, arms, and legs. Once again she was rescued by a fellow trainer, Terrill Jacobs. This incident marked the worst mauling of her long career and she was in and out of hospitals for the next two years. As soon as she could walk, she returned to the circus with her famous wild animal act. Now she seemed more fearless than ever and often, not always, entered the ring without a stick, blank pistol or whip. She would put the cats through their routine controlling them with her voice and attitude. The fact that the record shows she was hospitalized 18 times for injuries resulting from being mauled by these animals would indicate that perhaps she should have considered using some sort of defensive piece of equipment.

Mabel Stark's winter home was in Thousand Oaks, California, near Los Angeles, and in 1957, she was voted honorary mayor of the town. The town had a famous zoo and amusement park and Mabel performed there during the winter off-season. By 1960, she had retired from the road life of the circus and performed year-round at the park where, once again, she was the featured attraction. The park was renamed Jungleland and became a major attraction.

Stark was on top once again and she made frequent appearances on television. In 1968 the park was sold to a new owner who terminated Stark. Soon after her dismissal, one of her favorite tigers escaped from the Jungleland compound and was shot and killed. Mabel became very distraught over the loss of the animal, feeling if she had been there she could have persuaded the cat to return to its cage. Three months later she killed herself with an overdose of barbiturates. It was believed that the combination of being fired from her job, losing one of her beloved animals and no longer performing, caused the suicide. In the last pages of her autobiography "Hold That Tiger," Stark writes, "The chute door opens as I crack my whip and shout, Let them come! Out slink the striped cats, snarling, roaring, and leaping. It's a matchless thrill, and life without it is not worthwhile to me." Mabel Stark died at age 79, and she had been involved with wild animals, especially her favorite tigers, for 57 years. She is still considered the best female big cat trainer of all time.

Mabel Stark's act featured a tiger named Rajah that Stark adopted as a cub and raised in her apartment. Stark and the tiger performed incredible center ring acts for Ringling Brothers.

GUNTHER GEBEL-WILLIAMS

The wild animal trainer Gunther Gebel-Williams and promoter Irvin Felds are credited with revitalizing the circus in America during the 1970's. Gebel-Williams act featured all kinds of animals, elephants, tigers, lions, and horses. He just loved animals and the animals seemed to return the favor.

The wild animal trainer, Gunther Gebel-Williams, in combination with the entertainment promoter, Irving Feld, are credited with being responsible for revitalizing the circus in America. Feld bought Ringling Bros. from John Ringling North in 1968 for $8 million dollars. "The Greatest Show on

Earth" had been in a slow decline since 1950 as a result of stiff competition from movies and television, and absentee and lackadaisical management by the Ringling family. The spirit, style, and quality of the "Big One" was missing and the show was down to 12 acts.

Feld had spent his entire career in the entertainment business and he knew he needed to make a lot of improvements, but he definitely needed a star and a star act. For several years, Circus Williams and its owner and star Gunther Gebel-Williams had been the reigning champions of the European circus business. Circus Williams was a medium-sized circus with a big top holding 3500 people. John Ringling North had made several attempts to lure Gunther Gebel-Williams to America, but Williams always rejected the offers because he was busy building his own circus and had too many European ties. Irving Feld knew all of this and wisely decided to give Williams an offer he couldn't possibly refuse. Feld offered to buy the entire circus for $2 million dollars, just to get its superstar. The deal made Williams' foster mother a wealthy woman since she and her husband were the original owners and it gave Gunther the freedom to pursue his career in any direction he chose.

Gunther Gelbel-Williams was born in a small town in eastern Germany that is now part of Poland. The date was September 2, 1934, just as Adolf Hitler was assuming the role as head of Germany. When Germany went to war so did Gunther's father. He was sent to the eastern front, captured by the Russians, sent to the forced-labor camps in Siberia, and disappeared until 1949.

When the war ended, Gunther, his mother, and older sister fled the advancing Russian army and came to West Germany with absolutely nothing but what they could carry.

Gunther's mother needed to find a job to support the family. It happened that Circus Williams was starting up in the little town where the Gebels were staying. Mrs. Gebel saw an ad "Seamstress wanted" and she got the job. At this time, 1946, Gunther was 12 years old and his sister was 18. Since Mom had to travel with the circus, Gunther had to quit school and he never returned. His sister decided to get married and she pretty much disappeared from Gunther's life.

Circus Williams was a family business and many of the people had been circus folks for generations, only interrupted by the Second World War. These professionals took a real liking to young Gunther who appreciated their interest and was eager to learn the trade. Gunther's mother grew tired of all the continuous travelling and left the circus. Gunther loved the circus and stayed and the Williams family treated him like a son.

Herr Harry Williams, the circus owner and director, was an expert horseman, and he was already training his young daughter Jeanette to be the best equestrienne in the circus. Herr Williams not only taught young Gunther to be an expert rider, he also taught him his method for training animals.

In this case the animals happened to be horses, but the technique could be applied to any animal. Basically the method used by Herr Williams stressed patience above all else. He was methodically persistent in demonstrating whatever movement he wanted the horses to perform. Williams never struck an animal — no whip, no pistol, and no stick; instead he constantly repeated the instructions, using rewards for accomplishments, and mild rebukes for mistakes. It was pretty much the same approach used by Alfred Court at around the same time.

By the time Gunther was 16, Herr Williams let him begin driving horses in high-speed Roman style chariot races around the circus track. It was during one of these performances that Herr Williams was thrown from the chariot, hit his head and was killed. Mrs. Williams maiden name was Althoff, which was also an old German family circus name; so she had no trouble assuming control of the business. She asked Gunther, who was 17 at the time, to take control of the technical side of the operation. It was at this time that Frau Williams gave Gunther the family name and he became Gunther Gebel-Williams. The idea was the name would give him more authority when dealing with adults at his young age.

In 1960 Frau Williams married her daughter, Jeanette, to her adopted son, Gunther. By now Jeanette was a very accomplished star of the equestrienne show and Gunther was the operating head of the circus. Gunther commented years later that everyone thought it was a brilliant idea, but it didn't work because they were too much like "brother and sister". The marriage broke up in 1967, but the couple remained close friends for the rest of their lives.

At this time, Circus Williams began to prosper and Gunther began to win the biggest awards the circus world could offer. One year he was voted horseman of the year, the next year he was given a special honor for his herd of 20 performing elephants, and finally, three times in a row, he was elected "circus performer of the year". Gunther Gebel-Williams had hit the big time.

In 1968 Gebel-Williams married again to a woman he had spotted in the audience one afternoon. Sigrid was a blond, high fashion model with one child, she had been married once before. This was when Gunther decided to accept Irving

Feld's offer to leave for America and join Ringling Bros. circus. In addition to paying $2 million dollars for Circus Williams, Feld agreed to pay Gebel-Williams $1,000 per week for a minimum of five years. It turned out to be the best deal Irving Feld ever negotiated.

When Gunther Gebel-Williams opened the 99th edition of "The Greatest Show on Earth" in Madison Square Garden in 1969, he was an instant sensation. He appeared as the expert elephant trainer, the accomplished horseman and the amazing tiger trainer. He began a 20-year journey with Ringling's that established him as the greatest all-around star in circus history. He appeared in the steel cage with 17 tigers, and he introduced an elephant and two horses (all mortal enemies) to the act. He then appeared with his troupe of 20 trained elephants doing all sorts of stunts spread over all three rings. His feature elephant act was truly thrilling. An elephant runs from a standing start and stomps on the opposite end of a teeterboard, sending Gebel-Williams somersaulting through the air and landing upright on the back of another elephant. Of all the animals he trained, Gunther preferred elephants. He was quoted "You don't have to know me very long before you understand how much I love elephants. Elephants are very smart and very clever." Zoologists comparing animal intelligence rate only two animals higher than elephants — chimpanzees and orangutans. Elephants listen and they seem to enjoy doing what you tell them to do. Apparently, according to Gebel-Williams, there is no need to push them, or shove them, you just remind them of their act and they do it. He said that his elephants really enjoyed performing and showing off.

The teeterboard act became quite famous and was known as "Propulsion By Pachyderm Power". This elephant was one of Gunther's favorites, a female Indian elephant named Nellie. To illustrate Gunther's patience, friends claimed the elephant broke thousands of teeterboards before it developed the exact amount of pressure to apply to the board. Even after performing this stunt hundreds and hundreds of times every once in a while Nellie would have a relapse. The most memorable one occurred in the Baltimore Arena, when Nellie stomped on the board so hard it sent Gunther somersaulting to the top of the arena. The trapeze act netting that had been raised to be out of the way for Gunther's act saved him. He landed in the netting at the top of the arena, which had to be lowered to extricate him. Reaching the ground, Gunther exclaimed in his German/English, "I thought I was out of the building."

Gunther's horse act, was as impressive as the elephant act. He circled the track standing astride two Lipizzaner stallions followed by his wife, whom he had taught since their marriage, who was also standing astride two galloping Arabian stallions; the third performer was astride two more pure white stallions. This was, believe it or not, his first wife. The show, known as a "liberty horse act" began with wife number one in ring one, Gunther in ring two, and wife number two in ring three.

A "liberty horse act" means the horses perform without riders or reins using only verbal commands. They are "at liberty." Horses have been used to help establish this civilization of ours since the very beginning. Horses have a variety of attributes: they are strong and fast, their smell and hearing are superior to humans, and they have very good eyesight. The one characteristic where they fall painfully short is intelligence. Gunther Gebel-Williams began his career back in Germany at age 12 training horses. He always maintained that of all the animals he used—from leopards and giraffes to elephants—horses were the most difficult to train. He frequently said, "Horses are just not too bright." With this in mind imagine up to a dozen horses in each ring keeping time to the music and performing a host of intricate maneuvers in unison. These animals could rear on their hind legs, dance to the tune of a waltz or circle the ring weaving in and out of one another and then kneel and bow to the audience.

Of course, the center ring wild animals act was the featured performance because Gunther really loved tigers. Each year the act would change introducing a new incredible performance. To appreciate what this man accomplished you need to know a little bit about animals, but the basic fact is they are afraid of other animals, and they are all afraid of the tiger. The tiger is strong, quick, fast, very smart—and a carnivore—they eat other animals, including humans. The most amazing part of Gunther's wild animal act was the way he could mix wild animals in the same cage and then get them to perform stunts.

If you have ever owned a house cat and tried to train it to obey some simple commands, you will without a doubt, appreciate what it must take to train a dozen 500-pound Bengal tigers.

Gunther's wild animal act opened with 12 tigers in the center ring cage. These were absolutely gorgeous animals in the prime of their lives and each one is sitting on its assigned pedestal. As he calls their names, one by one, they leave their pedestals and line up in the center of the cage. At a barely noticeable command from Gunther, all 12 stand up on their hind legs and hold the pose for several seconds. Next comes a game of leap frog with one tiger leaping over another. Pretty soon the tigers are racing around the ring and each one is leaping over Gunther's head. The act continues for about 10 minutes and concludes with tigers jumping thru flaming hoops, another thing they are naturally very afraid even to be near.

As the show continued, Gunther's acts became more involved. It took him three years to develop the act featuring three tigers, two horses and an African elephant. The act was amazing for many reasons. First, of course, the horses and the elephant live in fear of the tiger. Next, the elephant was an African elephant, much larger than the Indian elephant, and distinguished by its large ears and tusks. African elephants are much more difficult to train than the Indian variety. Gunther began training this one, named Kongo, from the age of six months. The two horses he handpicked from a ranch in Waco, Texas. The three tigers were the toughest job. He and his wife, Sigrid, hand-raised and bottle-fed the three cubs from birth. When the cubs were six months old, Gunther began taking them on daily visits to Kongo and the two horses. After three years of daily training, this act was ready for the center ring. Part of the show featured one of the tigers riding on the elephant's back and another featured Gunther riding on the tiger.

In subsequent years, Gebel-Williams brought many more amazing wild animal acts to Ringling's center ring. One year he featured 15 leopards, three panthers and two pumas in the same cage, all of them swarming over Gunther's bare-chested body. He developed a trademark finale by parading around the hippodrome at the conclusion of his act with a spotted leopard draped around his shoulders. Gebel-Williams could accomplish all these magnificent feats with wild animals because of the rapport he established with the beasts.

Although part of his special ability was the result of an inborn genius with animals, his major attribute was the result of unbelievable patience and hard work.

Prior to each performance Gunther inspected each animal, checking their health and general well-being and most importantly, their mood. If anything did not look right, the animal was excused from performing. Following the performance the animals were fed personally by Gunther. An attendant accompanied Gunther with a wheelbarrow piled high with meat; one week they ate horse meat and the next week it was beef. At each cage he spoke to the tiger by name, opened the feeding door and tossed in a chunk of meat. He praised the ones that performed well and scolded the ones that did poorly. Gunther did this with Ringling's for 18 consecutive years, before taking a vacation to visit his aging mother in Germany and leaving his 16 year old son Mark in charge. In over a quarter century of appearing with Ringling Bros., Gunther never missed one of more than 12,000 performances.

His routine called for 16- hour days, seven days a week, eleven performances per week, 48 weeks per year for 22 years. Gunther had the physique and stamina of a top athlete with nerves of steel. At the top of his career, he was the highest paid performer in circus history and actually owned part of the circus. His act included 30 assistants, 21 elephants, 22 horses, 22 tigers, 3 camels, 2 llamas, 3 Shetland ponies and 12 Russian wolfhounds. This mix varied from year to year with giraffes, leopards, jaguars, etc. added or subtracted.

In 1995, Gunther was honored by Madison Square Garden for holding the record for most performances by an entertainer in the famous arena---1,191 appearances. Gunther and Irving Feld, the owner of Ringling Bros., became very close friends and remained that way for the rest of their lives. In addition, Jeanette, his first wife, and Gunther were close friends and star performers during their lengthy careers. Gunther and Sigrid raised two children, Tina and Mark who both became circus stars.

Gunther Gebel-Williams received many honors, was one of the few entertainers to become a legend in his own time, and was universally recognized as, "The Greatest Animal Trainer of All Time." He was featured in a CBS-TV network special, "Lord of the Rings" with Tony Curtis in 1977. Also a second special in 1981, the NBC-TV production, "My Father the Circus King, a behind the scenes look at Gunther through the eyes of his son, Mark Oliver Gebel, who became a featured animal trainer in his own right and starred with Ringling Bros. for many years. Gunther was a guest on many TV shows and one of the most memorable was an appearance with Johnny Carson on "The Tonight Show" where he brought along an elephant. His most recognized TV appearance was a commercial for American Express Credit Cards that featured Gunther with his favorite leopard, Kenny, draped across his shoulders. When Kenny eventually retired, Gunther attempted to replace him with a black 150- pound panther named "Zorro". Zorro was fine for a while but one day something disturbed him and he began hissing and snarling and clamped his teeth down on Gunther's head. Before being rushed to the hospital by ambulance, Gunther had to make sure Zorro was safely returned to his cage.

Gunther's 1989-90 Farewell Tour, broke all circus box office records as fans flocked to see him from the beginning in Venice, Florida to the final stop in Pittsburgh, PA., where he passed his boots to his son in a super-emotional ceremony. He became the manager of animals for Ringling's and returned to the circus ring for a limited 10- city tour in 1994, which served as the basis of a CBS-TV special, "The Return of Gunther Gebel-Williams."

In 1968, the circus was in a steep decline when Irving Feld, the brilliant and life-long entertainment entrepreneur, brought Gunther Gebel-Williams and his wild animals act to the U.S. to turn things around. From the moment in 1969 when he stepped into the center ring for the opening of the 99th edition of "The Greatest Show on Earth," he was destined to change the face of the American circus forever. His unique style and uncanny rapport with all animals created a new standard for all performers, not just in the circus, but also around the world. He always claimed he was an animal "trainer," not a "tamer." "I use only words, just words to train my animals. We are like a big family and we like and respect each other. I am the father and they are my children," he once said. Gunther Gebel-Williams demonstrated to everyone that humans and animals, all sorts of animals, could work, live and thrive together in harmony and banished forever the outdated notion that life is a case of "man or beast." He not only saved the circus, he changed the circus and everyone learned more about the beauty, nature and sheer splendor of the world's most interesting and exotic creatures.

In 2000, he was diagnosed with a cancerous brain tumor after feeling dizzy following a regular routine of feeding his animals at the Sarasota winter quarters. Gunther Gebel-Williams died July 2001, in Venice, Florida. He was 66 years old. In his memory, Ringling Bros., Barnum, and Bailey established the Gunther Gebel-Williams Foundation to honor his lifelong commitment to the partnership between humans and animals.

The Ringling Brothers circus parade featured a forty-horse hitch driven by Master Teamster Jake Posey and pulling the "Two Hemispheres" band wagon weighing seven tons and carrying 16 bandsmen. Compare this to the famous Budweiser team, which features six horses.

HORSES

The next feature on the program was that old mainstay of the circus, the equestrian act. Horses were a basic part of the traveling circus from the very beginning and they had two separate roles. For the first hundred years, until the 1930's, the horses did most of the heavy work. They pulled the wagons, loaded and unloaded the trains, along with the elephants they helped raise and lower the tents.

The horse's other role was as a performer and this role came in two versions, one without riders and one with riders showing their skills, as well as the talents of the horses.

It is not surprising that an audience around the turn of the century, 1900, would have a very special interest in horses. People were accustomed to horses, they appeared everywhere, every day, and the audience had the ability to appreciate the special skills of a horse or a rider.

In the year 1900, there were an estimated 20 million horses living in the U.S., and about three and a half million of these lived in cities. A few examples: New York City had about 100,000 horses, Rochester, New York had 15,000 and Chicago had 85,000. As a matter of interest, the pollution problem was major league. Each horse produced between 20 and 30 pounds of manure per day, the evidence of the horse was everywhere. Today there are about seven million horses in the United States. Prior to the arrival of the gasoline-powered vehicle, Ringling Bros. travelled with 750 horses, workhorses and performing horses combined. Feeding, transporting, caring, and cleaning-up for 750 large animals was a major task.

One of the most famous horse displays of the early circus took place in the circus parade, not under the tent at the circus grounds. Everyone is familiar today with the Anheuser Busch eight-horse hitch using Clydesdale horses. Anheuser Busch has three separate sets of these horses located around the U.S., and they appear in parades and various other events. The Clydesdales have become a trademark for Budweiser beer, AB's flagship brand, and they have appeared in print and TV advertising for years, winning many awards along the way.

When Ringling Bros. opened the 1903 season in New York City, the parade featured a 40-horse hitch driven by Master teamster Jake Posey, and pulling the new "Two Hemispheres" bandwagon, which was 36 feet long, weighed seven tons, and held 16 bandsmen. The bandwagon is on display as part of the Ringling Museum in Sarasota, Florida. The 40-horse hitch was harnessed in ten rows of four, the Percheron horses, each weighing about 2000 pounds, all wore brass-encrusted harnesses and giant red ear plumes.

Handling 40 horses and driving through major cities with many corners to turn was an unbelievable feat. The lead horses were 80 feet from the driver's box; there was no whip long enough to reach them. Posey kept the horses in line by voice signals and he knew the name of each one. This was not an easy task with a 16- piece band playing right behind him. Posey always had three men with him. One operated the wheel brakes, the second was available to quickly jump to the pavement to handle emergencies if a rein became snagged on a plume, a harness strap broke, or a barking dog was frightening the horses. The third man was the most important of the group; he sat directly behind Posy and fed the reins out or pulled them in as the team turned a corner. Turning a corner meant 20 feet of reins slipping thru Posey's fingers. Once the team turned the corner Posey had to pull the 20 feet of line back in so there would be no slack. Imagine the impression this feat made in the early 1900's on an audience that was thoroughly familiar with horses.

The equestrian acts in the circus were divided into three categories. Bareback riding involved men and women doing amazing acrobatic stunts on the backs of horses while they galloped around the ring. Some of these stunts involved leaping from one horse to another at full gallop, or as many as seven riders building a pyramid on the back of a moving horse.

Another equestrian act, known as high school or, "menage," involved displaying the skills of the horse or the horse and rider. This might involve the horse jumping over a series of six-foot fences or doing dance steps called the "Spanish-school." The third category called "voltage" involved a rider vaulting on and off a horses' back while it circled the ring.

The greatest equestrienne performers of all time was an Australian beauty named May Wirth, born June 6, 1894 in Bundaberg, Australia, the daughter of two impoverished itinerant circus performers. Her parents separated when she was seven years old and a sister of the Wirth brothers who operated the most successful circus in Australia adopted her. The sister's name was Maricka Wirth Martin, and she was considered one of the world's best equestriennes May had been performing as a contortionist and tight wire acrobat with the Wirth Bros. circus since the age of five and already knew how to do "flip flops." Once John and Maricka Martin adopted May her equestrian training began, and by the age of ten she was a major act, and at age 12 she received top billing. In 1911, when she was 17, Mrs. Martin brought May to the United States and she opened the 1912 season with the Barnum and Bailey Circus in Madison Square Garden. She was an instant sensation and the audience and the New York City press just fell in love with her. This peerless young woman, only five feet tall, with the patrician profile, was a perfect illustration of the equestrian art form—and she was really good!

May Wirth, an Australian beauty, was the greatest equestrienne in the history of the circus. She performed unbelievable acrobatics on the back of a horse. She could perform a backward somersault from one galloping horse to another trailing behind. May Wirth's act was the only one that all the other performers would gather in the tent to watch.

May Wirth, still a teenager, could do, with ease, things that few men had ever tried, and no woman had ever done. Somersaults were her specialty. She performed a back-backward somersault. Beginning with her back toward the galloping horse's head, so that she had to throw herself contrary to the forward motion of the steed, she would somersault into the air and twist simultaneously so that she landed on the back of the horse facing forward. Some of her other stunts included a forward somersault on a galloping horse, never performed by any female rider, somersaulting from one horse to another galloping alongside, and repeatedly jumping from the horse's back to the ground and leaping back up on the horse. But her greatest stunt involved somersaulting from the back of one horse onto the back of a horse trailing behind-- and doing this while the horses are galloping around the ring. These stunts became so well-known that she was required by her contract to perform them at each circus performance.

May Wirth became so good that the other circus performers would gather in the tent just to see her act. She began to add special little tricks to the routine just for the circus performers watching, knowing that most people in the audience could never appreciate their difficulty. One very special stunt involved three backward somersaults and one forward, in series, on a bareback galloping horse.

A measure of her fame came when she was severely injured on April 22, 1913; it was front-page news in the New York newspapers the next morning. Headlines proclaimed "Champion Bareback Rider of the World Seriously Injured" and "May Wirth Badly Hurt." The Barnum and Bailey Circus was playing in a tent in Brooklyn, New York, when the accident occurred. Fred Bradna, who was the head ringmaster for Ringling Bros. Barnum and Bailey for 40 years, described it as "the most heart- rending accident I have ever witnessed," and he had witnessed a lot of them. A newspaper account of the incident described it as follows: "Miss Wirth entered the center ring to do her act at 10:00 pm. She immediately received a thunderous ovation as she led off with a double somersault on the back of her horse. As she turned and bowed to the audience, her foot slipped and as she fell, her right foot became tangled in a rope stirrup used by circus attendants who cling to the horse as part of the performance. The frightened animal started on a wild dash around the ring dragging Miss Wirth through the cinders by her right leg. The horse, June, circled the ring five times with the rider's head hitting the wooden ring at least a dozen times before attendants could stop the animal. May Wirth was unconscious with a deep wound over her right ear and her body was a mass of bruises; but no broken bones."

The circus world thought she was finished at 18 years old. Her spirit was absolutely indomitable and she spent many months in rehabilitation. The following winter, nine months after the accident, she appeared before the Prince of Wales and the Queen Mother at a command performance at the Olympia London, on February 7, 1914.

May Wirth married long-time friend and fellow circus performer, Frank White, in 1919, and they settled in the Forest Hills section of New York City. May continued to perform receiving top billing in various vaudeville shows and circuses until her retirement from riding in 1937 at age 43.

May Wirth not only delighted audiences around the world for over 30 years, her daintiness and graciousness made her one of the most loved stars among her peer performers. She eventually completely retired from the circus business and moved to Sarasota, Florida where she died October 18, 1978. She was inducted into the Circus Hall of Fame in 1964 and remarks at the ceremony by the Ringling family described her as epitomizing the circus in its Golden Years. "She was a fascinating lady and there will never be another since her special art has disappeared from the entertainment scene."

My father, for all to see, was loving all the acts involving horses which were taking place in all three rings at the same time. One "over the top" act involved Ella Bradna's "Act Beautiful" and employed three white horses, 60 pigeons, 30 dogs, three clowns and 12 ballet girls as a backdrop for Ella's bareback ballet dance.

Another equestrian performance featured a family of seven riding teams of two, three, four, and five mounts, and eventually building a pyramid of all seven members galloping around the ring at full speed.

Other horse performances, going on simultaneously, included riders putting horses over six-foot jumps without holding the reins, just using their knees and heels. A Cossack demonstration where the riders jumped on and off the horses which were galloping at full speed, and a demonstration of high-school or "menage" riding where the horses execute exacting steps outlined by the Spanish school of horsemanship.

Finally, the equestrian "display" came to an end and we prepared for the "novelty" part of the performance.

The Zacchini family from Italy created the first successful cannonball act. The cannon shot the Zacchinis 70 feet into the air and a distance of 135 feet. Ringling Brothers continues today to shoot a young lady out of a cannon at every performance.

HUMAN CANNONBALL

Now the circus is noted for throwing superlative words around like adjectives; but the word used to describe the next "display" was spot on the mark, "exhilarating."

Some of the other commonly used terms to describe the acts included breathtaking, unbelievable, spectacular, enchanting, outrageous, thrilling, astounding, riveting, incredible, and awesome. Well this one was going to be exhilarating because a young woman was going to be shot out of a cannon. A bunch of horse acts was "ok" and interesting for the portion of the audience that understood and appreciated horses; but a human being shot out of a cannon, we are talking about some real excitement.

The human cannonball act was first performed in 1877, but it did not become popular until the Zacchini family arrived on the circus scene in 1922 with a cannon that used compressed air. The Zacchini family originated in Italy and the father invented the compressed air cannon and one of his sons, Hugo, became the first real "human cannonball." Hugo was born in 1898 in Peru, South America, where the family circus was on tour. Hugo grew up in his father's circus where he learned to perform juggling, trapeze, and other circus acts.

John Ringling, on one of his many talent-scouting trips to Europe, discovered Hugo performing his cannon ball act in Copenhagen, Denmark and offered him a contract to come to

America and perform with the Ringling Bros. and Barnum and Bailey Circus.

By 1930, the Zacchinis had perfected the act and were able to fire two of the sons simultaneously from a double cannon and they sailed across the arena together. The act was presented in a manner to make you believe these were regular cannons. The commands to fire were followed by a terrific explosion and a column of smoke as the bodies exited the mouth of the cannon on their flight across the arena. Of course, they were not "fired" like conventional explosive shells; they were pushed by compressed air which pushes a cylinder to the mouth of the cannon, similar to a catapult. The cannon shot the Zacchini brothers 70 feet up into the air and they travelled a lateral distance of 135 feet at an initial speed of 80 miles an hour before landing in a safety net. What has always made this stunt difficult as a travelling circus act is the math involved in calculating the force to use so the "cannonball" will land in the net. Heat and humidity play an important role in determining the distance a projectile will travel, and, of course, when the circus is appearing in indoor arenas, the allowable distance between the cannon and the net varies since the arena size varies. Miscalculating the amount of force to use by the smallest degree is the major risk associated with this act.

When the Zacchini sons went off to serve in the World War II they were replaced by women. Accidents did happen and on one occasion, the trajectories of the two "Human missiles" crossed and they collided in mid-flight. One of the girls broke her back and the other was very seriously injured.

The Zacchini family lived near Sarasota in the winter like most of the circus performers. Even in winter quarters, the various circus groups were separated. The management stayed in Sarasota where the Ringlings had their mansion, many of the performers chose Venice, while the sideshow personnel wound up in Gibsonton. The Zacchinis lived near Tampa. All of these people used the winter break to change or perfect their acts. The clowns worked on new gimmicks; the acrobats perfected feats that are even more daring; even the elephants, horses and tigers practiced their skills. Well, the Zacchinis were no exception and they had their two cannons set up in the backyard of their home. Since the yard was too small for the full trajectory of the cannons, they had to fire them across the road landing in a field down the street. Unsuspecting motorists would happen to witness this stunt and often lose control of their vehicle. After a number of accidents and incidents, the town, which treated the Zacchinis as a local marvel, erected signs at either end of the road announcing "If you see a flying man do not be alarmed. It is just the Zacchinis rehearsing their stunts." All the towns in the Sarasota area were very accommodating to circus personnel passing zoning laws that permitted elephants on the front lawns and trapeze equipment in the backyard, etc.

The cannonball act remains a staple of the circus and Ringling Bros currently employs two of the youngest female cannonball artists in the world, Elliana Grace and Gemma Kirby. These performers are an excellent illustration of being "born to the circus." Elliana Grace's mother founded Circus Harmony, a social circus school that uses circus arts to motivate social change. Growing up in Circus Harmony, Grace learned to perform balancing, acrobatic, aerial, and double trapeze acts. Gemma Kirby is a skilled dancer and trapeze artist, and was the valedictorian of her high school class before joining the circus. She's been launched out of the Ringling cannon over 300 times and she's just getting started.

Elliana and Gemma are launched out of a 24-foot cannon, fly to the very top of the arena, and land in a net 100 feet away.

Ringling Brothers continues to shoot a woman out of a cannon at each performance

BUFFALO BILL

In addition to horse acts, another staple of the early years of the circus was the "Wild West Show." Many of these shows were large enough to travel independently just like a regular circus; other smaller outfits were incorporated as acts in the larger circuses or frequently as a separate "after-show," or concert, in the main tent after the regular performance.

A typical Wild West Show included spectacular performances by sharpshooters, rough riders, cowboys, and Indians. Some of the famous movie cowboys began their careers with a travelling Wild West show: Tom Mix, William "Hopalong Cassidy" Boyd, and Tim McCoy, all began with the travelling western shows. Two authentic American heroes dominated this field of entertainment; Buffalo Bill and Annie Oakley.

Buffalo Bill was born as William Frederick Cody in Scott County, Iowa, on February 16, 1846. This guy grew up to become the "real thing". He embodied the Wild West, and became, not just an American hero, but an international star.

His father died when Bill was eleven and he immediately went to work to support his mother and sisters. His first job was as a messenger between wagon trains that were streaming across the western plains. When the Pony Express began operating in 1860, Bill Cody became a rider at the age of 14. At 15, he joined the Union army and served as a dispatch rider in the Kansas Cavalry. After the Civil War, he became a supplier of buffalo meat to the construction crews of the Union Pacific Railroad. His skill in slaughtering buffalo earned him the everlasting name of "Buffalo Bill."

Buffalo Bill Cody was the greatest star of the Wild West Shows that were popular in the late 1800's. He was a "real cowboy" and became the number one celebrity in America.

In the years of the truly wild west, Cody was in demand as a scout and guide for the U.S. Fifth Cavalry. Some gift of genius gave him practically total recall of all the western territory he had travelled since 1857. This skill was combined with expert marksmanship, a knowledge of Indian ways and terrific horse riding ability. In 1872, Cody was awarded America's highest military honor, the "Medal of Honor"; the award was later revoked in 1916 on the grounds that it was a military decoration, and Cody was a civilian employed by the military when he received it. His heroic exploits continued and the press back east just began to idolize him. In 1989, Congress re-instated the Medal of Honor awarded Cody.

The event that turned Cody into a full-blown sensation was the killing and scalping of the Cheyenne warrior known as "Yellow Hair." The event took place in Sioux County, Nebraska, on July 17, 1876, while the U.S. Army employed Cody as a scout, not a fighter. Yellow Hair challenged Cody to a duel that began on horseback and when both horses went down, they engaged in a pistol duel at 20 paces. Cody's bullet hit Yellow Hair in the chest, while Yellow Hair's bullet missed. Cody leaped on the Cheyenne warrior, drove his knife into the Indian's heart and then jerked his war bonnet off and scalped him in a period of about five seconds. Coming just three weeks after the massacre of General Custer and his entire force of 250 soldiers at Little Bighorn, Montana, Cody's feat had an enormous impact on the public's imagination.

After the Yellow Hair sensation, a promoter named Nathan Salsbury convinced Cody they could make a fortune with a "Wild West" show featuring Buffalo Bill. Salsbury was already a very successful promoter in the entertainment business.

The show organized by Cody and managed by Nathan Salsbury was an instant sensation. It opened with a "Grand Review" featuring 400 "Rough Riders of the World"-- Cowboys, Indians, Gauchos, Arabs, Scouts, Regular Soldier Cavalry from the armies of America, France, England, Germany, and Russia, all in their appropriate outfits.

The second act featured "Miss Annie Oakley, Celebrated Shot," demonstrating her dexterity in the use of firearms. This young lady could only be described as a "one-of-a-kind," absolute genius with firearms. The next chapter will discuss her show business career.

The show included 19 acts, but the highlight was "The Attack on the Deadwood Stage Coach by Indians." The coach became famous for making the death-defying run between Cheyenne, Wyoming and Deadwood, South Dakota. Gold had been discovered around Deadwood in the mid-1870's and the rush boosted the town's population to over 5,000, mostly men and prostitutes. The town had it all: gold, gambling, saloons, prostitutes, and guns--just no law and order. The stage often carried treasure and as a result, it was frequently a target of attacks by the Sioux Indians, and occasionally by bandits. Many people had lost their lives on the Deadwood stagecoach run and now Cody's Wild West Show had the very same coach as part of the show. The act was a real thriller with Indians galloping at full speed and the stage racing around the track, and everyone shooting and hollering. Then, of course, Buffalo Bill and his sidekick, Major Frank North, would ride in to save the stage and its occupants.

The show was the perfect attraction for the times and with Nathan Salsbury handling the finances it was an immense success here in America, and even more popular in

Europe. In 1887, the Jubilee Year of Britian's Queen Victoria, "Buffalo Bill's Wild West" played two command performances for the Queen. With that kind of royal reception, it was not surprising that over two- and a- half-million people attended the show during the London engagement alone. The next year the show played in Paris for six months, and in Rome, the Prince of Sermonetta challenged Cody's cowboys to tame his wild horses. The Prince's own horsemen had tried and failed and the challenge event attracted a crowd of 20,000 people. The horses were so wild a special outdoor steel reinforced arena had to be assembled. In practically no time at all, Buffalo Bill's Rough Riders had lassoed the horses, saddled, and mounted them. The spirited animals resisted in every way they could, but in a very short time the cowboys were riding them around the ring. The news of the speedy taming of the wildest horses in Europe by American cowboys spread quickly across the continent and the show became even more popular. Now Cody added an act where he and his cowboys offered to "break" and ride any horse offered to them, and they were always successful.

Nathan Salsbury became ill at the close of the 1894 season and the sickness made him an invalid for the rest of his life. Cody was a "showman extraordinaire," but as is so often the case, he had no business skills. He certainly had everything else; six feet tall, hair down to his shoulders, a classical nose and piercing brown eyes, incredible skills as both a marksman and a horseman, big time conservationist, close friend of the Indians, and a wonderful gift of charm. Everyone loved him, and he seemed to love them back. He was easily the number one celebrity in America.

With Salisbury out of the picture, the show began a slow but steady decline. In addition, Cody developed a serious drinking problem. He continued to be everyone's friend, often picking up the drinking tab with the last dollar in his pocket. Night after night, one of the show employees, Johnny Baker, who had joined the show as a kid and worshipped Buffalo Bill, would help his hero onto his horse. Cody would gather his courage and through sheer willpower enter the arena standing "tall in the saddle" and waving his big Stetson cowboy hat to the cheering crowd who had no idea they were seeing a mere shadow of the great man.

November 11, 1916 was his final show and he departed for his home in namesake Cody, Wyoming. Suffering from a bad cold and uremic poisoning, he travelled to Denver to be with his sister. William "Buffalo Bill" Cody died January 10th, 1917, a broke and defeated man. The entire nation mourned from President Theodore Roosevelt all the way to little school children who began sending pennies to erect a memorial. It was a most fortunate circumstance that the country chose to remember him for the great and talented human being he had been for most of his life, rather than the poor, pitiful man he had become. America honored "Buffalo Bill" as a real hero of the Wild West, they all loved him, whether they lived in New York City or Dodge City. He represented all the western ingredients that charmed people around the world: heroism, unlimited adventure and possibilities-- and he did it with a combination of courtly good looks, as well as openhearted and open-handed behavior that everyone truly loved. Cody was the subject of several movies, including the 1944 film, "Buffalo Bill," starring Joel McCrea and Maureen O'Hara.

ANNIE OAKLEY

When it comes to champions of the West, the undisputed female "champ" was a shy, little, five- foot, cute lady named Annie Oakley. Christened Phoebe Anne Oakley Moses at birth on August 13, 1860 in Woodland, Ohio, Annie had a real struggle in her early years. Her father died when she was six years old, her mother remarried and was widowed for a second time when Annie was nine years old. At the time of the second husband's death, the family was living in poverty and Annie and an older sister were sent to the local orphanage where she was placed in the care of the superintendent and his wife. At the age of ten she was 'bound out," to a local couple where she spent two years in near slavery conditions enduring both physical and mental abuse along with working unbelievable hours of physical labor. Annie later referred to the couple as "the wolves." Remember: she was only ten or eleven years old when this awful part of her life occurred. Annie eventually ran away, lived with another family for two years, and returned home at the age of fifteen. Her mother had remarried for the third time, but the family continued to live in poverty.

Annie Oakley had begun trapping and hunting small animals before she was seven years old. At the age of eight she was selling animals to the local meat market to help support her family. Later she sold game directly to restaurants and hotels in northern Ohio. When she returned home at the age of 15, her hunting skill paid off the mortgage on her mother's farm.

The undisputed female "Champion of the West" was Annie Oakley. Her marksmanship with a rifle or pistol was probably the best of all time. The famous musical "Annie Get Your Gun" is based on her life.

The big break for Annie Oakley came on Thanksgiving Day 1875 when the Baughman and Butler shooting show came to Cincinnati. Part of the show's attraction was always a side bet of $100 (worth over $2,000 today), that the show's sharpshooter star, Frank Butler, could beat any local fancy shooter. A Cincinnati hotel owner, Jack Frost, arranged a match between Annie and Frank Butler. The last opponent Butler ever expected to see was a five-foot-tall 15- year- old girl. The match involved shooting clay pigeons and after matching each other for 24 shots, Butler missed on the 25th turn.

The famous Irving Berlin musical about Annie Oakley includes the song "You Can't Get A Man With A Gun," however, following the famous match, Frank actually began courting Annie and they were married on August 26, 1876. Annie was 16 years old and the two of them stayed happily married the rest of their lives.

In 1885, Frank and Annie joined Buffalo Bill's Wild West Show and immediately became the show's most popular act. A typical show consisted of Annie shooting a cigarette out of Frank's mouth or a dime from between his fingers. She also did incredible backward shots where she sighted the target from a hand-held mirror and would shoot the cork out of a bottle at 90 feet. The most famous act involved using a .22 caliber rifle at 90 feet to split a playing card "edge on," and then put several more holes in it before it hit the ground.

This little lady, was probably the best shot with a rifle or pistol, of all time; and she did this without the aid of a scope and before the barrels of rifles and pistols had the precision machinery available today.

Annie and Frank joined Buffalo Bill's Wild West Show in 1885 and performed for the next 16 seasons including several in Europe where Annie became an international star. Frank eventually dropped out of the act and became Annie's manager. Other than Cody, Annie was the highest paid performer in the show and she and Frank became quite wealthy.

On October 29, 1901, the show was travelling on two separate trains near Danville, Virginia. Frank and Annie were on the second train, which, due to a misunderstanding at the switching station, ran head on into a southbound train. Annie was seriously injured and required five spinal operations and a lengthy rehab before recovering.

Annie was 41 years old and had been touring for 20 consecutive years, both in the U.S. and Europe. She decided to retire and pursue an acting career. She appeared in a play especially written for her, "The Western Girl," which put to use her talents for using a pistol, rifle, and rope. This touring show just added to her legend and celebrity status. As the leading female celebrity in the country, Annie continued to perform in exhibitions and charity events, particularly those involving women's rights. In late 1922, at a shooting contest in Pinehurst, N.C., the 62-year-old Oakley hit 100 clay targets in a row from 16 yards.

One famous true story describes an incident in Berlin where Crown Prince William asked her to shoot a cigarette held between his lips and she easily obliged. Later, when the Crown Prince became Kaiser Wilhelm and the First World War began in 1914, Annie was quoted as saying, "I sure wish I had missed that day." She did actually write him a letter asking for a second chance; no reply was received.

From the day she won the first shooting contest at age 15 until the very end, Annie Oakley remained true to her roots.

Fame, celebrity status bordering on worship, never changed her humble, charming, delightful personality.

Annie Oakley died on November 3, 1926, in Greenville, Ohio, at the age of 66. Frank, who sacrificed his own career and spent his life promoting his wife, and letting her shoot cigarettes out of his lips and from between his fingers, was so devastated, he stopped eating and died 18 days later on November 21st. They are buried in Greenville, Ohio. A vast collection of Annie Oakley's personal possessions, performance memorabilia, and firearms are on permanent exhibit at the Garst Museum and the National Annie Oakley Center in Greenville, Ohio. Upon their death, it was determined that Frank and Annie had donated most of their fortune to charity, particularly orphanages.

The movie, theatre, and TV industries have produced a lengthy number of shows describing the life of Annie Oakley.

The following is only a partial list of the more notable productions:

- 1935 movie "Annie Oakley" starring Barbara Stanwyck
- 1946 musical "Annie Get Your Gun" by Irving Berlin and starring Ethel Merman
- 1950 film version of the musical starring Betty Hutton and Howard Keel
- 1954-56 Annie Oakley television series starring Gail Davis

Numerous biographies and novels also describe her interesting life.

Unus was the stage name for Franz Furtner from Austria. The act featured Unus in the center ring in a three-ring display of hand balances. He would climb to the top of a large light bulb made especially for him by General Electric, and balance himself on his left index finger with his feet straight up in the air.

UNUS

The foundation of the circus depends on the all-time favorites: clowns, elephants, wild animal trainers and trapeze artists; but it takes a vast array of other acts to keep three rings and two stages occupied, non-stop, for two hours. This is where the circus athletes and novelty acts come into play, the leapers, tumblers, jugglers, balancers, trampoline artists, the girls in the aerial ballet, the thrilling perch act where the performers build a human pyramid three stories high, bicycle and motorcycle acts, and on and on it goes.

An Austrian using the name "Unus" performed certainly one of the most successful specialty acts in the history of the circus. John Ringling North saw the act in a Barcelona nightclub in 1946 and decided on the spot that he must add Unus to Ringling's circus. It was not easy persuading Franz Furtner, Unus' real name, to leave a pretty easy life touring Europe, staying in hotels and eating in fine restaurants, for a career of one-night stands, living in a railcar, performing and eating in a tent. But once again, as it usually does, money helped Franz make the decision to join the circus.

Franz Furtner was born October 19, 1907, in a small village in Austria. He began his adult life as a carpenter; but he began performing balancing acts and soon discovered he could make a living as a hand balancer. He chose the stage name "Unus," Latin meaning one or single, since the highlight of his act involved doing a "handstand" using only his forefinger for support.

By the time Ringling's brought Unus to America, 1948, he was already a superstar in Europe; and when he began performing here he was an immediate sensation. Then the Ringling Bros. advertising and publicity departments kicked into highgear and Unus was the star attraction of the circus.

The act featured Unus in the center ring in a three-ring display of hand balancers. For the finale of the act the spotlights converged on Unus wearing top hat and tails and white gloves. He would remove the gloves and show the audience his bare hands, replace the gloves and climb to the top of a large illuminated light bulb made especially for him by General Electric. On top of the bulb Unus would balance himself on his left index finger with his feet straight up in the air — a hand stand supported by only one index finger. Each time he performed this act the crowd would stand and cheer since it seemed simply impossible. How was he able to perform this amazing feat? Probably by combining his incredible equilibrist's skills with a little magic. It was often alleged that after showing his bare hands to the audience he would use sleight-of-hand to conceal a steel brace in his palm before putting the gloves back on his hands. You can conceive how closely observed he was night after night, especially in the winter when he travelled the vaudeville circuit with the nightclub audiences very close to the performance. No one was ever able to prove it wasn't the genuine thing. Unus stayed with Ringling Bros. for a few years, and then began appearing with Shrine Circuses, which were very popular in the 1950's and played extended performances in indoor arenas, no tents, and railcars.

Franz Furtner and his wife became American citizens, and settled, like most circus people, in Sarasota, Florida. They had three daughters and a son. One daughter, Victoria, attended Sarasota High School, which had begun a circus program in 1949 as an offshoot of its gymnastics classes.

Unus's daughter Victoria, also became a superstar with Ringling Brothers and has been inducted into the Circus Hall of Fame.

The Sarasota Sailor Circus continues to operate today, over 60 successful years later. Victoria, or Vicky, joined the Sailor Circus program at age 15 and by the time she graduated, she was the featured star of the show. After graduating from high school in 1963 at the age of 18, she debuted at Madison Square Garden with Ringling Bros. She was given a big pre-debut build-up by Ringling's press corps who promised that a new star would emerge under the "Big

Top" of the "Greatest Show on Earth." Originally billed as "La Toria," Victoria fulfilled her potential as an aerialist and became a true circus star. Her performance included acts of amazing skill and strength, including aerial splits, handstands and various other poses, while hanging onto a rope 70 feet up in the air. Her featured act involved looping, one-arm swings, where she hung by one arm from a Roman Ring high above the circus floor and flung her body up, and over in a rotating fashion while the audience counted the full rotations. Her record was 250 revolutions. The act, known as the "plange," was made famous 50 years earlier by the circus star Lilian Lietzel. Vicky Unus performed for 20 years during the 60's and 70's, and retired in her prime at 40 years old.

The year Vicky debuted with Ringling Bros, 1963, "Unus the Great" retired. He was inducted into both the "Circus Ring of Fame" in St. Albans Circle near Sarasota, and the "Circus Hall of Fame" in Peru, Indiana. Vicky Unus was inducted into Sarasota's Circus Ring of Fame in 2005. Unus died in 1994 at age 87 and his daughter lives in Sarasota.

The Sarasota High School Sailor Circus has become a prestigious training ground for future performers in the many circus arts, from jugglers and clowns, to acrobats and aerialists. Drawing on the circus heritage of the Sarasota area and the many retired performers living nearby, the school is able to offer a level of instruction not available anywhere else. Public performances are scheduled each spring during the annual holiday, and over the past 65 years over a million people have attended the event.

THE SHOW

The circus program described the center ring feature acts, and the total was 23 "displays," about normal for a typical circus. In addition, associated acts were performing simultaneously in the adjacent two rings and the stages between the rings. With the music blaring, the clowns performing mischief around the track, "candy butchers" shouting their wares, the accomplished announcer introducing and describing each act in dramatic fashion and 12,000 people shouting, laughing, screaming, and applauding, the tent was an exciting place to be, especially if you were ten years old.

With five separate and thoroughly exciting acts performing at one time, and the acts changing completely about every ten minutes, the place was an absolute marvel of organization. All these performers and animals and their accompanying costumes and equipment, had to be entering and exiting the tent precisely on cue while the band and the announcer kept pace in this non-stop "Greatest Show On Earth."

There were dogs playing dominoes with perfect politeness. Ponies walked on their hind legs carrying schoolbooks and later executed a precise military drill; while a trained rat climbed a pole and raised the American flag. The "Learned Pig" could pick out the letters PIG from a jumble of alphabet cards, stand on his hind legs, take a bow, and then sit at a table and play a game of poker with a fellow pig.

Meanwhile, the domino-playing dogs appeared to drop dead only to be revived into a dancing frenzy by a monkey playing a fiddle. Other animals were enjoying a game of soccer, playing musical instruments and riding bicycles. Consider the training and patience required to teach these animals to perform these stunts. Two goats played seesaw with one continually bouncing the other off the end of the board. Bears dressed like humans were riding motorcycles, and elephants were busy painting canvases with their trunks, spinning hoops or lifting pretty ladies to ride on their backs.

These acts are just a sampling of the mayhem going on in the three rings and two stages---and this only describes some of the animal acts; there were also many, many human "displays."

The human performers included jugglers doing incredible stunts with everything from glass vases to flaming torches, motorcycles, three of them, zipping around a metal sphere about 15-feet in diameter, tumblers, teeterboard artists, 40 aerial ballet artists — and that is only a partial list of the dazzling performances. All performed accompanied by wonderful music and wearing beautiful costumes. All this action was necessary because it was always an unwritten rule: "A pause is the worst thing that can happen to a circus performance."

The next featured acts were the most thrilling for me and involved the trapeze artists or "flyers" as they are known in the circus. The show had opened for almost an hour and a half with the Wallendas high- wire bicycle and pyramid act and now it was time for "the daring young man on the flying trapeze, he flies through the air with the greatest of ease." The song was written and published in 1867, and the lyrics were based on the phenomenal success of French trapeze artist Jules Leotard, who is credited with inventing the flying trapeze. Born in Toulouse, France, in 1836, Leotard studied to become a lawyer. At 18 years of age, he began experimenting with bars, ropes, and rings suspended over a swimming pool. The same year Leotard invented the trapeze, 1859, another Frenchman, Jean-Gravelet (Blondin) crossed Niagara Falls on a tightrope.

Leotard is most famous for inventing the one-piece streamlined garment that bears his name. The outfit was designed to improve safety and agility for the trapeze performer; but became more noteworthy for its ability to show off the acrobat's physique and impress the ladies in the audience. Today the leotard is the name for tight-fitting, female athletic garments. Sadly, Jules Leotard died at the young age of 32, probably from smallpox.

The trapeze act in the circus has several variations requiring different skills. Solo acts on the trapeze include standing on one's head on the trapeze bar while it swings back and forth at the very top of the tent or auditorium, or hanging by the heels and performing almost unbelievable acrobatic stunts. Many of the artists performing these acts are contortionists as well as acrobats, and this skill really enhances the performance.

Eddie and Ira Milkte, father and son, performed one of the most dangerous spectacles ever developed for the trapeze. The pair performed on a single trapeze 70 feet in the air under roof, and 55 feet under canvas, without a net. The act involved the pair standing on their heads on the trapeze bar while it swings back and forth in a wide arc. They drank water, smoked cigarettes, while upside down and swinging, and many other unnerving stunts. All these routines were done in perfect unison and the finale was absolutely breathtaking. Picture this: with the trapeze swinging at its fullest arc, Eddie, the father, stood on the bar without holding on to the ropes. Then, Ira climbed on Eddie's shoulders, and, upside down, stood on Eddie's head; they were head to head swinging the full arc of the trapeze at the top of the tent -- without a net. For 13 years between 1917 and 1930, this act reigned supreme among the many aerial acts of the circus.

In the circus world, the folks who fly through the air or "flyers" perform with those who catch them called "catchers." These people are the top athletes in the circus world and the profession requires a rare combination of strength, coordination, and skill. Most of the people who succeed at this profession are from circus families; their parents are performers and able to begin teaching the children at an early age. This is not a vocation you would choose to pursue later in life.

The "basic" trapeze performance consists of a flyer standing on a platform, and as far away as practical across the tent, the catcher is ready; each performer grabs a swinging trapeze and the catcher is now hanging by his legs, head down, poised to catch the flyer who leaves his trapeze and flies across the space between the two. Perfect co-ordination is necessary between catcher and flyer, and if anything goes wrong, only the catcher is in a position to correct the timing by changing the speed of his trapeze or the amount of his arm's extension. The contact between the catcher and the flyer is a perfect locking of each other's hands to each other's wrists. An important variable in the act is the combination of the weight and speed of the flyer. A light feminine flyer performing a regular routine is a completely different situation than catching a heavier male athlete at the end of a triple somersault.

During the 1920's and 30's the skills of the trapeze artists grew and the first addition to the act was known as the "flying return." The flyer would leave his swinging trapeze at the top of its arc, plummet down to be caught by the catcher who would fling him back toward the empty trapeze. Grabbing the trapeze with perfect timing, the flyer would return to the platform (pedestal) that he had left just moments before. One of the best displays of this act involved the Silbon family. Using three catchers and six flyers, the air at the top of the tent was filled with flying bodies. Three flyers soaring toward the catchers, their empty trapezes seized by three others making a flying return.

The next development to the routine involved the flyer performing acrobatic stunts in mid-air on the flight from the trapeze to the catcher. The most frequent stunt was the somersault, which soon became a double somersault, and then the quest for the elusive triple somersault began.

The superstar, Alfredo Codona, discussed earlier with his wife Lilian Leitzel, became the first to perfect the triple somersault while flying from a trapeze to a catcher. Cordona was quoted from an interview in 1930 with the Saturday Evening Post, a leading national magazine for many years. "My job with the Ringling Brothers and Barnum and Bailey Circus hinges upon the fact that I can be depended upon twice daily, rain or shine, to turn a triple somersault from a trapeze into the waiting hands of my brother Lalo. My speed, when I leave the trapeze for the triple has been accurately measured; I am travelling at the rate of 62 miles an hour. At that speed I must turn completely over three times, in a space not more than seven feet square, and break out of my revolutions at precisely the instant that will land me into the hands of Lalo, who, hanging to his trapeze by his ankles, has swung forward to meet me."

Once, Alfredo misjudged the timing leaving the trapeze bar by less than one hundredth of a second and was four inches off target. Alfredro's head struck Lalo in the chin knocking him unconscious from the catch bar. Alfredo landed face down in the safety net-- next, Lalo, still unconscious, fell on Alfredo's back breaking five of Alfredo's ribs.

Alfredo Codona is considered the greatest trapeze artist of all time. The product of a circus family in Mexico, his flying career began at age five.

Alfredo had another stunning trick where he swung the trapeze to its very highest arc, then shot over the bar, curved into the air, straightened out, and dived like a bullet into the net. Two feet before striking the net, he would go into a forward somersault. On one occasion, he went straight through the rotting net. This unbelievably superb athlete described the moment of the life-threatening incident. "I was about eight feet off the ground and in a position that meant certain death. In that eight feet I jerked out of the forward somersault into a backward one, lit on my feet instantly turning three more somersaults, a succession of roll-overs and came to my feet for my bow to the audience, absolutely uninjured". He also personally sought out the property man responsible for hanging a rotting net and severely dealt with that problem.

On July 12, 1982, performing under the bright spotlights of the Tucson (Arizona) Community Center, Miquel Vasquez, a 17 year-old member of the Flying Vasquez team, became the first aerialist to perform the quadruple somersault, a goal that had eluded "flyers" since Alfredo Codona began performing the "triple" in the 1920's.

Hurling thru the air at 75 miles per hour, Miquel was caught by his 31-year-old brother, Juan, who was hanging upside down, by his ankles, from the other trapeze bar. The two brothers performed the stunt thousands of times from 1982 to 1994. They continue to be involved in the production of circus acts in Las Vegas.

Alfredro Cordona was considered the greatest flyer of all time, and Antoinette Concello was the best female flyer to ever appear in a circus. Antoinette Comeau was born in Sutton, Quebec of French-Canadian parents. Her older sister, Mickey, was already appearing as a trapeze artist with the

Sells Floto Circus when Antoinette joined her during her summer vacation from a convent in Vermont. Antoinette never returned to the convent, she was 16 years old. It was 1928, and following a summer travelling with the circus she was sent to the Eddie and Mayme Ward flying school in Bloomington, Illinois, the premier flying school at the time. She had extraordinary skills from the beginning and progressed rapidly, learning to be a catcher, then mastering all the "picture tricks" and the important maneuver of how to tumble into the net. This is an important skill, since a fall on the head would usually break your neck. The technique involves keeping the arms close to the body, and chin down tight to the collarbone, and directing the weight to land on the shoulders and hips.

Antoinette spent another summer touring with the circus and appearing in the trapeze act. In the winter, she returned to the Ward's school in Bloomington where Arthur Concello, their most promising student, was also training. The two became close friends, Arthur was training to achieve the triple somersault, and Antoinette was trying for the double. The two flyers married and formed the Flying Concellos Act, which employed two flyers working from a single trapeze— one grasping it as the other left it.

Antoinette and Arthur eventually purchased the Ward's school and continued to perfect their act. The great day came with the 1937 opening of Ringling Bros. in Madison Square Garden when Antoinette and Arthur Concello performed the "triple" on the same bill. This was the highest form of team-flying ever performed.

Antoinette went on to become the undisputed "greatest female flyer of all time." In 1956, the Concellos divorced and two years later injuries force her to retire to Sarasota and raise her son. Ringling's called her out of retirement to return to the circus and serve as aerial director of the show, which included 70 aerial ballet artists. She won several circus hall of fame awards and died at her home in Sarasota on February 5th, 1984.

Arthur Concello was not just an accomplished performer and circus star. He was also a genius at managing the circus. Ownership of several circuses and partnerships with Ringling Bros. made Arthur Concello a very wealthy man. He is credited with inventing a portable, collapsible steel grandstand mounted on mechanized trailers, which saved a huge amount of time and labor erecting seating for thousands of circus spectators. He was a partner with Cecile B DeMille in producing the blockbuster 1952 movie, "The Greatest Show on Earth" staring Charlton Heston and Betty Hutton. Incidentally, Antoinette Concello was responsible for training Betty Hutton for her trapeze artist role. The film won several Academy Awards and made a ton of money. Arthur Concello died July 4th, 2001, at the age 89 in Sarasota, Florida. He will be remembered as an all-star circus performer, and, perhaps, more importantly as a business genius whose logistics skills were able to streamline the circus and keep it afloat for many years. In 1947, John Ringling North, President of Ringling Bros., appointed Concello general manager of the circus and he held that position for many years guiding Ringling Bros, from a giant, lumbering, traveling tent show to a streamlined, moneymaking spectacle playing existing outdoor and indoor arenas around the United States.

Back to Olean: the show had begun over two hours ago with a high-wire act featuring the "Flying Wallendas" and now it was about to end with another high-wire spectacle. Ringling's employed over 70 ballet girls who performed a variety of acts that included complex dance routines, riding the elephants, and performing aerial ballet, as well as singing in the chorus. Most of these talented beauties had been hired from the New York Theater (Broadway), where they were temporarily out of work and waiting for the next big opportunity. Imagine 70 to 80 young ladies living in very close quarters, on the move every night, surviving on two buckets of water a day in a communal dressing tent   Living conditions on the train were primitive and congested. The Single Ladies Car, commonly called "The Virgin's Car" by the circus workers, often held four berths per section, although designed for only two people, thus doubling the capacity of a normal Pullman car. The four lavatories at the end of the car had no walls; management had them removed to prevent monopolizing them. To maintain order each car had a supervisor and a porter. The porter polished shoes every day, handled the laundry once a week, and cleaned the sleeping births. Each of the girls was expected to tip him 25cents per week.

Complaints abounded! The food was too fattening, the costumes were unflattering, and the shoes didn't fit. In addition, they were often homesick and jealous, and frequent minor spats developed with each other. They were all anxious to leave the circus at the first rumor of a Broadway curtain call for a new play.

And there was another troublesome ingredient at work with these young ladies: the so-called "stage mother". These young, beautiful, potential "stars," had mothers who hung around the circus backyard acting as diligent guardians of their daughter's professional and moral reputations. Fred Bradna, the Ringling show boss for many years, is quoted as saying to Clyde Beatty that he should replace his lions, tigers and leopards with 16 of these stage mothers in the big cage and he would have the most ferocious , clawing, and certainly the noisiest cat act of all time.

These young ladies may not have been completely happy, and they were working hard for very little pay; but, they were performing, and that is what they wanted to do. They performed twice each day before an audience of 12,000 people in every major city in America.

The aerial ballet act was not "a piece of cake." It took training, skill and more than a little courage to climb a rope up to 50 feet in the air, then begin doing a routine of spins, and ankle and wrists holds, some upside down; all without a net. All of this aerial ballet activity with accompanying loud, but very good, band music was only a distraction for the event about to occur above the center ring, the tight wire act was about to begin.

During the 1920's and 30's one young lady was responsible for making this act a big part of the circus. Considered to be the most beautiful circus performer of all time, Bird Millman performed on the tight- wire high above the center ring. Born Jennadean Engleman in Canon City, Colorado, population 2500, on October 20, 1890, this girl became famous around the world. She began her career as a precocious child performer and worked her way up from small-town travelling circuses to the big-time vaudeville circuits performing with her parents as the Millman Trio. She was so dainty her father gave her the nickname "Bird." In 1913 she signed with Ringling Bros. and immediately became a super-star attraction. Bird Millman was petite, with short brown hair parted high and drawn over her left ear with a barrette; she was vivacious and charming and enjoyed flirting with the audience.

177

When Bird Millman would begin her performance, accompanied by not just the circus band but a mixed chorus of eight voices, all other activity in the Big Top came to a halt. The other two rings and stages were empty, and the candy butchers ceased shouting their wares--a rare event for Ringling Bros.

At the top of the tent, on wire 36-feet long, twice as long as all other wire artists used, the darling of the Jazz Age would begin her song and dance routine. She was the first tight- wire artist to work without an umbrella or balancing pole. She would dance the waltz, cakewalk and two-step; accompanied by the chorus and singing herself. Her best number was a Hawaiian dance on the high wire while the chorus sang "Aloha." All these acts were not extremely difficult, that was not what made her a superstar, it was her personality; she had the hypnotic charm of a true star. She would be singing "Tip-toe Through the Tulips" or "Would You Like to Spoon With Me" while carrying a small balloon and performing leaps and pirouettes as though she were on a ballet stage, not a tight- wire high in the air. For a finish, she would race at full speed from one end of the wire to the other, jump through a paper hoop, and land on the pedestal.

Bird Millman stayed busy year round, appearing with the Ziegfeld Follies during the winter months or travelling the European vaudeville circuit, where she became a world-famous personality. She captured everyone's attention in 1917 by performing one of her more famous stunts. Bird donated her services to the government by performing on a wire strung between two New York City skyscrapers 25 stories in the air. The act was a publicity stunt to aid the Liberty Loan Drive at the beginning of America's involvement in the First

World War. Bird went on to appear in several Broadway plays and a several movies.

She was one of the highest paid entertainers in the world, and certainly one of the most famous; but Bird Millman never changed. She remained dainty and gracious and simply loved to entertain. A wonderful quote by one of the newspaper columnists sums up her popularity. He said, "If, when I die, I get to heaven, Bird Millman will be the first person I would like to meet."

Sadly, Bird's private life did not match the success of her public one. Her first marriage was a brief one and it was annulled. The second marriage was also short and ended in a divorce. Finally, in 1924, she found and married the man of her dreams; millionaire Harvard graduate, Joseph O'Day. She happily retired determined to make this marriage work. Unfortunately, within a few years the stock market crash of 1929 wiped out both their fortunes. O'Day died three months later and Bird was left destitute and had to return to Colorado to live with her family. Bird Millman died August 8th, 1940, of cancer. She was 49 years old.

The 21st and last "display" known as the Grand Finale was about to be announced. During World War II, the government felt the circus played a vital role in lifting spirits and morale, especially in rural America; and, as a result, despite rationing, allowed the circus to continue to travel and perform at "full speed."

The closing act titled "The Circus Salutes America" was an all-out patriotic bombshell. Behold the 36-piece band blaring one patriotic song after another, colorful spotlights circling the tent, cannons firing round blanks, a huge parade of all the performers in red, white and blue costumes, and to top it off, the elephants assembled in the three rings waving

American flags with their trunks. It was supposed to be spectacular, and it definitely filled the bill!

In the "Roaring 20's" the aerialist, Bird Millman, became one of the most famous and highly paid entertainers in the world. Her popularity is demonstrated by a quote from a newspaper columnist, "If, when I die, I get to heaven, Bird Millman will be the first person I would like to meet."

THE TEARDOWN

As we began to exit the tent with 12,000 other people, another absolute miracle of efficiency was about to take place, known in the circus as "the tear down." In fact, it had already been taking place since we entered the Big Top over two hours earlier.

The first tent, with equipment and personnel, to leave was the dining tent, which left the grounds shortly after the last meal was served, around seven pm. Subsequently, each tent that was no longer needed for the show was taken down, packed up, and hauled off to the waiting railcars. These early-to- leave groups included the blacksmith, the harness maker, the so-called "rest tents," the three ticket-seller wagons, and all the concession stands. As the evening progressed, and the show began under the Big Top, the sideshow and the menagerie tents came down and were taken to the train. By the time the evening performance ended, 10:30pm, only the Big Top and the dressing room tents remained standing.

When the show ended, the "canvas bossman" blew his whistle and 110 canvass workers swarmed over the Big Top, each doing his assigned task. This entire job of removing the aerialists' rigging took less than two hours; taking down all the lights, packing up chairs and bleachers seating 12,000 people, lowering the canvass and rolling each section into bundles, pulling the main poles, quarter poles, side poles and hundreds and hundreds of stakes; and loading all this in the proper sequence on designated wagons. The canvass alone weighed 18 tons when dry; after a rain, it weighed three and one-half times as much, 63 tons. Think of doing this in a rainstorm, which seemed to happen often.

The rail siding was a beehive of activity under a blaze of floodlights. There were 60 drivers that operated the trucks that towed the wagons to and from the circus lot, and another 60 men assigned to the very dangerous job of loading the wagons on and off the railroad flatcars. This task was the source of many serious accidents, 50 of these wagons were loaded with animals, many of them considered wild and dangerous. The elephants were usually the last to arrive at the railyard, and by this time, the first two trains had already left for the next town. The 50 elephants usually walked to the train accompanied by their handlers, which numbered about 60 men.

The entire task of taking the Big Top down and packing all the bleachers and equipment on wagons took less than two hours.

THE BACK LOT

Usually the circus travelled eight months, opening in April at New York's Madison Square Garden and closing in a southern city on the way back to winter quarters in Sarasota, Florida. The season would last about 220 days and during this time, the circus would travel over 13,000 miles, visit over 100 cities, and play over 400 performances. It is an amazing feat that this traveling city with over 1,500 people, hundreds of animals, countless trucks, wagons, tents and other paraphernalia, could do this, rest for four months, and then repeat the same routine the next year. This unusual business, which was highly profitable for the owners, required a combination of the best organization, expert management and a core of dedicated employees, some with very special skills. The unique living conditions of the circus actually contributed to its success. The constant travelling afforded little opportunity to generate friendships with anyone except fellow employees. And the caste system, described earlier, further limited your exposure. The circus backlot, or backyard, and the circus winter quarters offered two special opportunities to socialize with fellow circus employees and their families.

The circus set up over 40 tents at each of the more than 100 stops on a typical year's route; but the public usually was admitted to only the sideshow and menagerie tents, and, of course, the Big Top. The rest of the tents comprised the "backlot" of the circus, and were considered the private backyard of the employees.

This young lady is shown on the back lot carrying two of the water buckets allotted to each performer.

On a clear and sunny day, the backlot could be a very busy place. Behind all the show business glamour, all the participants had to take care of daily life. Hair had to be washed and tinted, broken saddles and other equipment repaired, babies had to be fed, laundry washed and pressed, and older children had to be home-schooled. Horses were being "shoed" in the blacksmith's tent. The barber was busy in his tent; the medical tent, staffed by a doctor and nurses, was always busy, as were the veterinarian's quarters. Amid all this well-organized activity, the mailman was making his rounds along with the circus chaplain. Father Ed Sullivan was the legendary chaplain of the circus for decades. Father Sullivan, a Roman Catholic priest from Boston, began travelling with the circus in 1928 and continued for 40 years. Father Jerry Hogan was the next circus chaplain, and he continued the practice of treating the circus like a travelling parish: conducting mass, performing weddings and baptisms, and perhaps, most importantly, listening to people's problems, which can be many when living this type of existence. In other areas of the lot someone might be touching up a wagon, others were gambling or playing chess. One of the most important activities taking place was the age-old custom of circus families' children "learning the ropes." This is where the family kept the traditions alive for generations-- where the trapeze artist learned to fly, the bareback rider began riding, and the acrobat learned all the stunts of the trade.

Socialization took place in the dining tent, the dressing tents, the rest tents, and the private tents of some of the star performers. The special circus caste system was alive and well even on the backlot. The clowns had their own "clown alley", the workers or "roustabouts" slept or rested in or on the wagons. The sideshow performers, unusual people even by circus standards, were completely separated from the rest of the employees. A trapeze artist, ballet girl or bareback equestrienne could be with the show for several seasons and never make contact with the fire eater, sword swallower or the fat lady. The sideshow performers travelled in a separate railcar, even dined at different hours, performed in a separate tent and were confined to a special area on the backlot. Even the folks who ran the "midway," the concessionaires or "candy butchers," kept to themselves during the very little free time they had available.

Showgirls ready to enter the "Big Top" for the matinee performance.

Of course, the management was at the top of the system and only mingled with fellow managers or the stars of the show. The routine performers did not have an abundance of spare time since they appeared throughout the show. Following breakfast they washed clothes, worked on their routines or made a quick trip into town if it were within walking distance. The matinee performance began at 2:00 pm and lasted over two hours. Dinner was served between 5 and 6:30 pm, and the evening show began promptly at 8:00 pm and usually lasted until at least 10:30. Since the performer's exposure was limited to a very small group, and for short periods of time, these people often became extremely close friends with very little contact outside the circus.

One other special characteristic had a big impact on this environment: in an average year, a large circus like Ringling Bros employed performers from over 30 countries. Not only did this result in a variety of cultural differences, more importantly, it involved many languages being spoken. To make the situation even more complex, these performers were usually from circus families, home schooled with a limited education and often only spoke their native language, not English. However, it is true that some of the performers, especially the stars from European countries, spoke English and several other languages. One thing that made Fred Bradna, director of Ringling Bros. for 40 years so successful, was being fluent in six languages. This foreign language barrier was just one more item that served to shrink the size of the personal contact base in the circus backlot.

It is not surprising that the children of circus families growing up in such close contact every day for eight months each year with these unusually talented people eventually became circus people of some sort themselves Almost every star described in this book had an early association with the circus. They may have started out as a bare-back rider or a juggler or tumbler and wound up as a clown, but the circus was in their blood or bones or genes.

The circus workers (roustabouts), the men who labored unloading the trains and putting the tents up and down, were not long-term employees. Ringling's and the other large operations had a small cadre of skilled permanent employees who were mainstays of the show; they knew how to load and unload a train of wild animals, install 12,000 seats in two hours and raise a huge tent in a driving rainstorm. The other 1,000 employees who manned the sledgehammers, pulled on the ropes and pushed the wagons had to be recruited each spring. Since this was not permanent work and offered no income over the four winter months; the job attracted a rootless, reckless, tough, anonymous type of individual. They usually had no family and few, if any, friends; they had no loyalty to the circus or anything else. They lacked the capacity or the desire, or maybe both, to enter the regular workforce. It doesn't take much imagination to see that 1,000 men of this caliber, living the nomadic life the circus offered, was a pretty good recipe for some sort of trouble every day.

The surprising thing is that it all worked quite well, and moving each day probably contributed to keeping possible disruptions to a minimum. Still, admittedly, there was an abundance of gambling and fighting, and an absence of basic hygiene and cleanliness. One method management employed to keep this situation under control was the use of private detectives, such as the Pinkerton or Burns Agencies. These people were able to spot particularly disruptive individuals and bodily remove them from the circus. This was necessary because the whole operation depended on precise scheduling; the tent had to go up on time or the show would not begin on time, and it also had to be down on time or the train would not be on schedule.

The personnel who ran this operation had to be experienced and tough but also needed to be expert managers of a difficult group of people. Most of all they had to be dedicated to the circus. It is surprising, even amazing, how many people, both management and performers, stayed with the circus, usually the same circus, their entire careers. This was not an easy life; eight months on the road living in a tent and sleeping in a railcar. All sorts of weather prevailed; rain and wind to heat and cold---without air conditioning or heaters. Wind was a particularly dangerous event for the circus and they had special procedures for handling what was termed a "blowdown." Handling 40 tents in a surprise 60–mile-an hour windstorm is a challenge. One of the often used techniques for dealing with a storm involved shortening the performance significantly. Once again the circus had special terms for this situation: a "John Robinson" or a "Quick Show" was a performance cut to the bare minimum to get the crowd out ahead of the storm.

But long-termers like Fred Bradna, the ringmaster or equestrian director, stayed with Ringling Bros.travelling every season with his performing wife Ella. Lou Jacobs, the clown, performed with Ringling's for 60 years and Merle Evans, the talented band director, a very demanding job twice each day, performed with Ringling Bros. from 1919 to his retirement in 1969, over 50 years. Alice from Dallas, the famous sideshow fat lady, weighed 628 pounds, and toured with Ringling's for 30 years. Imagine being that heavy and travelling with the circus for 30 years—and she was married to the same man the whole time.

Performing "not so glamorous" chores on the circus backlot.

The circus used another practice to encourage employees to stay for the entire season. A "gratuity" or "holdback" was retained as part of the weekly wages; this was not returned to the worker until the end of the season, and, of course, the amount held back grew larger each week. This practice was also used to enforce the many rules the management imposed on the employees. There were rules forbidding drinking, smoking, gambling, and swearing; standards for cleanliness and dress were established; and there were policies against the ballet girls fraternizing with male performers or any townspeople. Fred Bradna was promoted to equestrian director because the previous director eloped with a ballet girl. One of the methods used to enforce these many rules was to fine the employee and deduct the amount from his "holdback" pay. In addition to rules discouraging lower level circus employees from fraternizing with people in the town they were visiting, the circus people in general did not feel comfortable with "outsiders." They even had nicknames for noncircus folk: "rubes" or "gullies" were circus terms for outsiders.

So, despite all the restrictions imposed by the circus caste system, the language barriers and the nomadic life style of one-night stands show people saw themselves as part of a closely knit travelling community. Within small groups, they slept together, ate together, and performed together and spent most of their limited spare time with the same people. A real sense of solidarity developed within the clown group, the equestrians, the ballet, and showgirls and especially among the sideshow performers. Despite the rules and social barriers, a lot of romance took place on the backlot and a significant portion of these closely-knit groups consisted of families with children. The sideshow folks created some odd combinations. Al Tomaini was over eight feet tall, wore size 27 shoes, and appeared with Ringling's as the "giant" for many years. His wife, Jeanie, was approximately two and one-half feet tall and toured the sideshow circuit as the "half-woman."

An old vaudeville joke may shed light on the performers' love of their circus. Seems one of the roustabouts longed to be in the show, and worked his way up to a role in the animal clean-up crew. One day, after cleaning elephant manure for several hours, he confided in a co-worker, "This is a terrible job." The friend asked, "Why don't you quit and get another job?"

The clean-up worker answered, "What? And leave show business?!?"

Afternoon activities between shows on the backlot of the Ringling Brothers Circus.

WINTER QUARTERS

Baraboo, Wisconsin was the original winter quarters for Ringling Brothers and is home for the Circus World Museum and the Al Ringling Theater

In late November of each year, when the circus stopped travelling, it returned to "winter quarters." For many years, Ringling's wintered in Bridgeport, Connecticut; but in 1927, John Ringling moved the quarters to Sarasota, Florida where he had built a mansion and where he had extensive real estate holdings. The new winter quarters opened to visitors on Christmas Day 1927. Families were invited to see circus rehearsals as well as animals from all over the world. The winter quarters became one of Florida's top tourist attractions. The quarters occupied what had been the county fairgrounds and spread over many adjacent acres. There were tents, menageries, practice rings, workshops and a rail yard for the four trains.

When the circus stopped touring the employees had to make some tough decisions since they stopped being paid, as well as not being housed and fed. The lower- rung people (roustabouts, ballet girls, dining tent employees) had to search for other employment. Some of the performers went on tour with vaudeville shows, especially in Europe; but the bulk of the show people followed the circus to Florida.

Once again, the sideshow folks, or "freaks," remained separated from the main body of the show; they settled in a town about midway between Sarasota and Tampa. The first sideshow performers to settle in Gibsonton, Florida, were Al Tomainio, the giant, and his wife Jeanie, the half woman; the two of them ran a very popular fishing camp. When the circus winter quarters moved to Sarasota, Gibsonton, also known as "Gibtown," "Showtown," or "Carny Town", became a mecca for people who didn't quite fit anywhere else. It wasn't very long before we had an American town where the mayor was a midget and the fire chief was a giant. Siamese twin sisters ran a fruit stand and people were training wild animals in their front yards. The post office had a counter for midgets and the bar had special chairs for the "fat lady" and the "giant." On a trip into town you might meet Percilla the "Monkey Girl", the "Lobster Boy" or the "Anatomical Wonder", as well as a fire eater, sword swallower or human pincushion.

The Showtown Bar in Gibsonton, Florida continues to operate today. In the mid-1900's it was the gathering spot for all the sideshow performers that lived in Gibsonton during the winter.

Unique zoning laws, called "Business Residential," permitted residents to keep everything from elephants to circus trailers on their property. The Showtown bar and restaurant was the main gathering place; and karaoke night every Wednesday with this reservoir of talent was a "sight to behold". It was here at the Showtown Lounge where Melvin Burkhart livened up the bar crowd by hammering six-inch spikes up his nose. Melvin was billed on the road as "the Human Blockhead" and he had an assortment of bizarre stunts that comprised his carnival act.

In 1992, Gibsonton was hit with some negative publicity when the "Lobster Boy," a.k.a. Grady Stiles, was murdered. Stiles was the fourth generation in his family to be born with deformed hands that resembled claws and legs that looked like flippers. Two of his four children had the same defect.

195

Grady Stiles was married three times to two women; he drank too much, and was frequently accused of abusing his family. When his oldest daughter announced she was getting married, Stiles shot and killed her fiancé the night before the wedding. He was found guilty of murder, but the court did not send him to prison stating that the State of Florida prison system could not accommodate his physical needs. The famous "Lobster Boy" was sentenced to 15 years of probation. Then, years later, in 1992, following years of abuse, his wife, Mary Theresa, asked their son-in-law to help her escape from her husband. The solution came with three shots to Stiles' head while he sat watching television. The son-in-law was found guilty and sentenced to life in prison. Mary Theresa was sentenced to 12 years in prison; but she always claimed she only did what was necessary to protect her family. Justice often works in mysterious ways.

The International Independent Showmen's Association, established in 1966, is headquartered in Gibsonton. It is nonprofit and is the largest showmen's association in the United States with over 4500 members in the outdoor amusement industry. The club grounds serve as host to the largest trade show in the carnival industry during February each year. The event serves as a fundraiser for the IISA and the money is donated to charitable organizations and scholarships in the outdoor amusement business. So, if you are in the market for a new Ferris wheel, or just something for the backyard, like a merry-go-round or a chair-o-plane, this is your place.

The International Independent Showmen's Association also sponsors a unique museum located in Gibsonton. The museum features memorabilia from the history of the American Carnival, circus midway, and travelling shows. In addition to a 52,000 square foot building, there is an outdoor exhibit of show wagons, midway rides and other carnival apparatus, including the trailers used by the performers who travelled with the shows. One of the very first Ferris wheels is on display and operating. You can see one of burlesque performer Gypsy Rose Lee's slinky black-beaded costumes that shocked people when she performed with the great Royal American Shows Carnival. The outfit worn by the "Viking Giant," Johanon J. Petursson, is on display. The giant was nearly nine feet tall and weighed 425 pounds. The boots he wore daily are the size of a small child, and you could fit a half dollar through one of the rings he wore. The museum has thousands of posters and photographs depicting the early traveling shows and circuses that brought the main, and often, the only, entertainment to rural America 100 years ago.

This museum brings the old-time carnival to life with Tilt-A-Whirl rides, a whole row featuring games of chance, (Fisher-Fisher and Spill the Milk), concessions, (cotton candy and corn dogs), the freaks, and the girlie shows. The museum has a recording of the actual spiel used by the barker to attract people to the burlesque show. With the girls on the stage, it sounds like this: "Take a good look at these costumes folks. Once you get inside you'll never see them again. Here's Tammy from Miami, the girl with the million-dollar treasure chest. You'll have your hands in your pockets and a new grip on life. Don't look for grandpa, he's already inside."

There is a wonderful miniature carnival on display featuring 15,000 little people standing in line at over 275 concession stands, ogling 74 separate exhibits, and riding the 127 miniature rides. Today Gibsonton, located 15 miles south of Tampa, is home to about 14,000 people and some remnants of its carnival heyday survive. There is a monument to the

"Giant" with a replica of one of his boots on the top; yards are still littered with old carnival trailers and rides' sort of a status symbol in this town; and you can still get a drink in the famous Showtown Bar.

Sarasota remained the Ringling Bros. winter quarters for over 30 years and many smaller shows followed their lead and moved to the area. In 1960, Ringling's moved the winter quarters to nearby Venice, Florida where it remained until the railroad stopped running there in 1992. The new home was in Tampa and it has moved several times since to Plantation and Ellenton, Florida, both in the Tampa area.

All this circus activity in the Sarasota region over the past 100 years has made the area a mecca for circus fans. There are circus museums, circus schools and shows; and most importantly, you'll find a treasure of retired and active circus and carnival performers who work hard to keep the tradition alive.

A few other American towns have a claim to circus history. Baraboo, Wisconsin, the birthplace of the seven Ringling brothers, and the "original" winter quarters, is home to the Circus World Museum and the Al Ringling Theatre, an active landmark in the city.

The Circus World Museum was built in 1884 and designated a National Historical Site in 1969. The museum is owned by the Wisconsin Historical Society and operated by the Circus World Museum Foundation. The museum occupies the grounds and eight of the ten original buildings used as the winter headquarters of the Ringling Brothers Circus from 1884 to 1918. The buildings include the Ring Barn, Elephant House, Animal House, Baggage House Barn, Winter Quarters Office, and the Wardrobe Department. In addition to the original buildings, the Irvin Feld Exhibit Hall, the museum's largest building, houses exhibits from the Ringling Brothers Circus, as well as other displays relating to general aspects of circus history.

The museum has a permanent big-top that is used for the daily circus and magic show performances. The W. W. Depp Wagon Pavilion houses a wonderful collection of 50 colorfully decorated and carefully restored antique circus wagons. The C. P. Fox Wagon Restoration Center is used by the museum to restore circus wagons to their past glory and visitors are welcome to view the restoration work in progress. Finally, the Robert L. Parkinson Library and Research Center is a research facility holding collections of circus- related books, photographs, archives and periodicals, and is open to the public at no charge.

The Great Circus Parade, sponsored by the Circus World Museum, is a parade of marching bands, circus wagons, clowns, performers, and animals. The parade is a re-creation of the parades that preceded the performance when the circus came to town in the late 19th and early 20th centuries. It was first held in Milwaukee, Wisconsin in 1963 and between 1980 and 2009 it was held in Milwaukee, Chicago, and Baraboo, Wisconsin. Plans are to hold the parade every few years in the future. The parade is a big one, and includes over 30 marching bands, 50 circus wagons, 400 horses, and other animals, and many colorful floats with clowns and performers. A steam operated calliope "brings up the rear" of the several hour-long spectacle.

Peru, a small town located in north central Indiana, is the home of the International Circus Hall of Fame, which has also been designated a National Historic Landmark. From 1914 to the 1930's, Peru was the winter headquarters for many major circuses, including Sells-Floto and Hagenbeck and Wallace, two of the largest shows at the time. Located on the original winter quarters lot, the Hall of Fame Museum has a display of circus wagons, posters, photos and other circus related paraphernalia. There is a miniature replica of the complete Hagenbeck and Wallace Circus of 1934, which includes all of the performers, animals, wagons, and even the entire circus parade.

In July each year, this place comes alive with celebrations, parades, and circus performances featuring both young amateurs and professional stars from around the world. Peru is home to the only remaining calliope manufacturer in the United States.

Peru, Indiana is the home of the Circus Hall Of Fame.

TROUBLED TIMES

Following the end of the World War II a big competitor for the entertainment dollar was introduced to the American audience. Television became the major factor in the decline of the traditional circus in America. The Age of Television dawned faster than anyone could have anticipated.

In September 1947, for the first time, people in major cities could watch the World Series on TV. Of course, they had to view it in a club or a bar as TV sets had not made it into the home as yet. Living in Olean, New York, a small town (21,000 people), nestled in the hills of western New York State; we had to drive to the top of Rock City Mountain where a bar/restaurant had a tower to receive the TV signal from the Buffalo stations. By 1949, two years later, there were one million TV sets in the United States, and just 10 years later, there were over 50 million in operation. Today there are 285 million television sets operating in over 115 million American homes. It wasn't just the circus that suffered from this period of the 1950's, over 5,000 movie theaters also closed.

There were a few other factors that hastened the decline of the Big Top. A basic reason the tent show had to go was simply stated "there was no place to put it." Ringling Bros. had 41 tents that required a minimum of 15 acres to set up, and another adjacent huge area to park at least 3,000 automobiles. There was nowhere in the United States with a 20-acre vacant lot within walking distance of downtown or located conveniently close to public transportation. As the 1950's wore on, the major circuses began to go bankrupt.

By the mid 1950's, there were only five medium to big circuses touring the United States: Ringling Brothers and Barnum and Bailey, Clyde Beatty Shows, Kelly-Miller, Mills Brothers and Christians Bros. Circus. The major Cole Bros. Show had already gone bankrupt soon to be followed by the Kelly-Miller Circus and several others.

On July 16, 1956, in Pittsburgh, Pennsylvania, after the evening performance, Ringling Bros ended its tour in mid-season and returned to winter quarters in Sarasota, Fl. It wasn't just TV that was bringing the circus down; other issues were also having a major negative economic impact. Working conditions and pay for circus employees had never been outstanding or even average. The International Brotherhood of Teamsters Union proposed they become the sole bargaining agent for all non-performing Ringling personnel, and they presented the president of Ringling's, John Ringling North, with a contract. North rejected the contract saying the circus couldn't afford it. The head of the Teamsters Union was Jimmy Hoffa, a tough, corrupt, mafia-related union boss, and not someone to be treated lightly. He personally vowed to put Ringling Bros. out of business. The result was a campaign of constant harassment, slow-downs, picket lines, sabotage, etc. In addition to these problems, the big railroads, once a friendly ally of the circus, now found the big circus trains nothing but an irritant. In the ten -year period following the end of the World War II, the railroads increased charges for moving the circus train by 250 percent.

IRVIN FELD

In 1967, the sale of Ringling Brothers by John Ringling North to Irvin Feld (on right) was celebrated with a lion cub in the Roman Colosseum. The Ringling family had operated the circus for 83 years. The Feld family has run Ringling Brothers continuously since 1967.

Into this depressing scene stepped Irvin Feld who thought he knew how to arrange a comeback for the circus in America. Feld had contacted John Ringling North six months prior to the final show in Pittsburgh with his plan for saving the circus. North's response was to ignore the letter. Now, six months later, the day after the Big Top folded, North telephoned Feld and told him he was ready to listen to his ideas.

The story of Feld is one of those truly, and typically American business success stories. Feld was born in Hagerstown, Maryland on May 9th, 1918. His father was Jewish and had emigrated to the United States to flee the prejudice in Russia. By the time the 1930's Depression arrived, Ike Feld had six children to support on a modest income from a clothing store in downtown Hagerstown. When the store went bankrupt, Irvin was 13 and his older brother Izzy was 21. They had to earn some money, so they went on the road selling "snake oil" at summer carnivals. Their route covered the low mountains north of Hagerstown and into southern Pennsylvania. The towns were small hamlets, remote and poor. They had names like Yellow Creek, Stone Gap, Walnut Bottom, and Beaver Town. Many of these places had absolutely no entertainment, not even a movie theater. The summer carnival visit with its medicine show was the highlight of the year.

Before we proceed any further with the interesting story of the Feld brothers, a brief explanation of the popular travelling medicine show will be worthwhile. Medicine shows travelled the summer carnival circuit by truck, horse, or wagon, and peddled a "miracle cure" between various entertainment acts. The "miracle elixir", (sometimes indelicately referred to as "snake oil"), was usually claimed to cure any disease, remove stains, prolong life, smooth wrinkles or help with any other problem that might be troubling you. Most shows had their own special patent medicine, (the medicines were not patented, but it sounded more official). Entertainment included just about anything: a juggler, a freak show, jokes, storytelling or magic tricks. The man running the show posed as a doctor and he drew the crowd with an over-the-top spiel. The entertainment kept the crowd around until the "doctor" sold the medicine. Sometimes people bought it just to show their appreciation for the free entertainment.

So, while Izzy sold the snake oil and collected the money, Irvin was the "pitchman" with a spiel that would have made P.T. Barnum proud. Irvin was also part of the entertainment, launching into a terrifying account of the difficulty and danger associated with capturing just the right snakes to produce this special patented blend. Actually the stuff was from a supply house in Baltimore and the Felds never knew exactly what it was; but from this day on the two brothers were a team. The ideas usually came from Irvin and to make them work financially was Izzy's department. They saved $500.00 for the family that summer and the next year their show was bigger and fancier, topped off by a red- and-yellow striped awning.

In 1939, the Baltimore supply house that supplied the snake oil loaned the Feld brothers $1,000 to open a variety store in a Washington, D.C. black neighborhood. Shortly after opening, the NACCP urged the Felds to expand the store to include a drugstore and luncheonette. They did this by leasing the drugstore to a black pharmacist, and giving the city of Washington its first integrated lunch counter.

Irvin Feld always thought "big" and always felt "big is better." The next thing he did turned out to be a game-changer. He opened a record shop in the back of the store, and a few years later he had a chain of record stores. This little operation put the Feld brothers in the music business. Using the music knowledge, along with the travelling carnival experience from their early years, they managed to enter the music tour business. They were pioneers in packaging rock- and -roll tours for the most popular artists of the time: Chubby Checkers, Frankie Avalon, Fabian, Everly Brothers, and Buddy Holly. Irvin is credited with discovering a 15- year- old Canadian boy who had composed and sung a song called "Diane." Feld became his personal manager, handled the publicity and promotion, put him on tour, and shared in the fortune that Paul Anka would make as a singer and composer.

Now, as a result of all this work, the Feld brothers had acquired an intimate knowledge of the entertainment business throughout the United States They were especially well-versed regarding the location of the many new air-conditioned and heated indoor auditoriums that had been built since the end of the war. Feld felt that this knowledge, plus his booking know-how, could be the solution of the Ringling Bros. Circus problems.

The first thing Irvin Feld told John Ringling North and his staff was that the circus was engaged in six different businesses. First, they were in the construction business because they erected a virtual tent city every day and tore it down every night. This required hundreds of people. They were in the restaurant business since they fed 1300 people three meals each day for eight months; this meant serving 900,000 meals a year. The hotel business had to be part of the operation since sleeping accommodations were provided for 1300 people. The circus had been able to downsize from 1,500 due to the increased use of trucks and tractors replacing wagons. They were even in the sanitation business because it was necessary to provide restrooms for the thousands of people attending the circus as well as the workers and the performers. It was also necessary to clean up after all the circus animals. Of course, they were in the railroad business owning over 100 rail cars, many of them specially designed; and travelling 20,000 miles a year. And, finally, they were in the entertainment business, and that was the only one of the six that made money.

Feld proposed that North drop all the businesses except the show business. Irvin Feld offered the following deal: North's only obligation would be to deliver the circus to the locations that Feld had booked. The Felds would have complete control over bookings and promotions. They would be responsible for paying all rentals and advertising charges. They also guaranteed that operating the circus would not exceed a certain maximum figure each week. The Felds also recommended dropping the menagerie and the sideshow because they were outdated. It was a very big change. Now the show's equipment moved by truck, the performers were given a travel allowance, and they ate in restaurants and slept in hotels. They used their own vehicles to get from town to town. The elephants and other animals still travelled by train, which now only had 15 cars. Another advantage, since the circus was playing in almost all indoor auditoriums, the season was extended from the first week of January to the third week of November.

The next ten years were not good for the circus business. There were five large shows and several smaller ones on tour, and although they were "hanging in there", they were barely making a profit. As a result, the quality of all the shows declined to a dismal level. Ringling Bros. Greatest Show On Earth was reduced to a dozen acts from the historical norm of 21 displays. John Ringling North, president of Ringling's for 40 years, nephew of John Ringling, became disinterested in the circus business, moved to Switzerland in 1962, where he remained the rest of his life.

On January 1st, 1967, Irvin Feld made a New Year's resolution. He would either acquire Ringling Brothers that year or he would sever all his connections with the operation. The decline of the whole show reached a point where Feld was actually ashamed to be associated with it. He later stated that owning the circus became an obsession with him. So, on the first day of January 1967, Feld phoned North and told him they needed to talk about the circus. They met at the Excelsior Hotel in Rome and Feld presented his proposal to buy the circus. John Ringling loved the circus and, prior to 1962, he had worked hard to make it successful thru good times and bad. The Ringling family had owned the circus for 83 years.

Finally, North agreed to sell the circus for $7.5 million; but he wanted it all in cash---"not one cent in a note." Negotiations dragged on until November when Irvin Feld was back in Rome with his brother Izzy, and a partner, Judge Roy Hofheinz, builder of the Houston Astrodome, America's largest indoor arena at the time. The final price was $8 million. Prior to Judge Hofheinz, Feld had lined up another partner who thought he could talk North into reducing the price. North's immediate reaction to this overture was to consider it an insult, and raise the price a half a million dollars. Feld arranged a publicity stunt worthy of the great P.T. Barnum by having the deal finalized in the ancient

Roman Colosseum with John Ringling North holding a baby lion cub.

The Feld brothers purchasing The Greatest Show on Earth was not welcomed by the circus family, those people who "belonged" to the circus. These were the folks that were born to the circus, worked it their entire lives, and had a distrust that troupers have for towners. They also claimed that the Felds had never trouped with a circus-- they were, " money men" who had bought their way, not earned the right way, into the circus. The Felds would prove them wrong.

The first big change didn't happen until the 1969 season. Feld announced that there would be two separate, but equal, shows on tour for the '69 season, a red unit and a blue unit. One new show would be produced each year and run for two years; it would be with the blue unit for one year and switch to the red unit the next year. Since the red and blue units travelled separate routes, the scheduled cities would have a new show every year. Even though the season had been lengthened to eleven months a year, Feld believed there were more profitable show dates available than the circus could handle in a season. Just about everyone was opposed to the radical idea, including his own employees and John Ringling North, who threatened to remove the Ringling name from the show. North's question was "How can there be two "Greatest Shows on Earth," —which one will really be the greatest?" Feld's answer was "both." 50 years later, The Greatest Show on Earth travels the U.S. with a red and a blue unit.

Feld had another serious problem, his greatest competition for being the first to introduce European and South American circus acts to the American audience was a very popular Sunday night TV show, "The Ed Sullivan Show." Feld would fly to Europe a minimum of six times a year to personally scout for talent and beat Sullivan to the acts.

In 1968, everyone in show business knew the premier act in the world was Germany's Gunther Gebel-Williams. As discussed earlier in this book, North had attempted to persuade Gunther to come to America on several occasions, but he had a host of reasons for not wanting to leave Circus Williams. Feld solved the problem by simply buying the entire circus for the staggering sum of two million dollars. What a wise investment this was for the Feld Brothers. Gunther Gebel-Williams turned out to be the greatest all-around star in circus history. From his first American tour with Ringling Brothers in 1969, the comeback of the circus in America was guaranteed.

The Feld brothers decided Ringling Brothers performers had grown a little old for a profession that relies on physical skills and where beauty has always been a major feature. The facts showed the average age of a performer with Ringling's was 46, and many of the showgirls were in their fifties. The clowns had dwindled from over 50 in the circus heyday to 13 in 1968, seven were in their 70's and 80's and the youngest was over 50. Feld decided to establish the Ringling Brothers, Barnum, and Bailey Clown College in Venice, Florida. This school was a big hit and at one time, it could boast that there were so many applicants that its acceptance rate was lower than Harvard's. The school trained over 1,400 clowns over a 30- year span and flourished until 1997. The closing was due to the fact the school was no longer necessary. With over 1,400 graduates, the profession was wellstaffed, and these clowns were teaching others the lessons they had learned.

In 1971, the Felds sold Ringling Brothers and Barnum and Bailey Circus to the Mattel Toy Co, for $47 million. The very lucrative concessions and command over the production of the performances remained with the Felds. Ten years later, March 1982, the Felds bought the circus back for far less than it had sold for in 1971--$22.8 million. Mattel was never able to exploit the synergy of the toy line with the circus the way Disney combines the movie hits with the theme parks. Feld also acquired Ice Follies, Holiday on Ice and Disney's World On Ice.

Irvin Feld passed away in 1984, and was inducted into the Circus Hall of Fame in 1987. His brother Israel (Izzy) had died in 1972. In 1970, Irvin's son Kenneth joined the firm and he became president in 1984 after his father's death. Feld Entertainment was organized in 1996 and now conducts a worldwide business with operations in over 50 countries. In addition to Ringling Brothers Circus, and the other entertainment shows, it has added a Motor Sports Division that operates Monster Jam, Supercross and several other truck -related attractions. Other divisions of the company operate live touring shows for Disney, and the Feld Consumer Products Division handles concessions and merchandising worldwide. Kenneth Feld's daughters, executive vice-presidents of the company, Nicole and Alana Feld, handle the production of the Ringling Brothers and Barnum and Bailey Circus. In 2016 the red and blue division's titles, "Circus Extreme" and "Built to Amaze," are touring America coast to coast, the 145th year for Ringling Brothers.

The acrobats performing for Cirque du Soleil are simply dazzling.

CIRQUE DU SOLEIL

Guy Laliberte from Quebec, Canada founded Cirque du Soleil in 1984. Today it is the largest theatrical entertainment company in the world and Laliberte is one of the wealthiest people on the planet.

Cirque du Soleil, "Circus of the Sun," is the largest theatrical entertainment company in the world. It was founded in Baie-Saint Paul, Quebec, Canada in 1984 by two street performers, Guy Laliberte and Gilles Ste-Croix.

Guy Laliberte quit school and left home at age 18 to pursue "some sort of performing career." He toured Europe for a while as a folk musician and also learned the art of "fire breathing." In the summer of 1979, he met Daniel Gauthier and Gilles Ste-Croix who were managing a youth hostel for performing artists in Baie-Saint Paul. The trio decided to turn the group staying at the youth hostel and themselves into an organized performing troupe. In a publicity stunt to obtain funds to start the troupe, Ste-Croix walked from Baie-Saint Paul to Quecbec City on stilts, a distance of 56 miles. The stunt caught the attention of the Quebec Provincial government, which provided necessary funding.

The troupe, using the name "Les Echassiers," (The Waders), toured Quebec in the summer of 1980 and the show was a success with audience and critics. Unfortunately, it was a financial failure. For the next few years, Laliberte and Ste-Croix organized a summer arts fair in Baie-Saint Paul and toured the local area. The big break came in 1983 when the Canada Counsel for the Arts gave them a grant of $1.5 million to host a production the following year-- as part of Quebec's celebration of the 450th anniversary of the French explorer Jacque Cartier's voyage to Canada. Laliberte named the show he created for the celebration "Le Grand Tour du Circus du Soleil."

What made this show special is the character-driven approach to the performances and the complete absence of animals. This style has become known as the "nouveau cirque," or the "contemporary circus." Each show has its own central theme and story line. Cirque du Soleil has a few other defining characteristics: shows employ continuous, non-stop, live music; there are no stagehands, performers change the props, and there is only one ring. The show depends on feats of human skill and daring performed in, above and around a ring, counterpointed by the antics and tricks of clowns, jugglers and magicians. A typical show consists of acrobats, aerialists, trick bicyclists, jugglers, contortionists, teeterboard flippers and clowns. These performers are at the top of their game, the very best. Denis Lacombe is rated as one of the top clowns in the past 100 years. Lacombe produced a clown act for the 1988 Cirque du Soleil tour that features him as the mad conductor of Tchaikovsky's "1812 Overture." During the five-minute performance, he almost disappears under an avalanche of sheet music; conducts in a totally horizontal position while somehow his feet remain attached to the podium, then pulls an endless supply of batons from his pants-- and in a violent finish, loses his pants and the shirtsleeves of his jacket, almost disappears into the podium only to reappear for a final flourish. Over the years, this act has made Denis Lacombe quite famous as one of the best clowns of the past century.

By 1990, Cirque du Soleil was making money at a rate that allowed it to create additional shows and now it retires older shows and opens new ones every year. It currently has 18 permanent and touring shows in operation, some of them have been going strong for over 20 years. La Nouba premiered in its own building at Disney, Orlando, Florida, in December 1998, and has been pretty much sold out ever since. There are eight permanent shows playing in Las Vegas to a total audience of over 10,000 people each night. These permanent, called "resident," shows last 90 minutes without interruption. The touring shows usually have two 50 -minute acts with a 30- minute intermission.

Cirque du Soleil touring shows travel under the title "Grand Chapiteau," (Big Top), and are easily recognized by their distinctive blue and yellow colors. The infrastructure that travels with each show would certainly remind you of the circus in its heyday. In addition to the Grand Chapiteau, there is a large entrance tent, an artistic tent, a kitchen, a school, and just about everything else needed to support the cast and the crew. The kitchen serves 250 meals each day, the Big Top is 60 feet high and 167 feet in diameter and seats 2,000 spectators. It takes eight days to set up the tents and the show and three days to take it down and pack it into the travel containers. Depending upon the show, it takes 50 to 75 tractor-trailer trucks to transport all the tents and equipment. They even have their own power source provided by five diesel generators.

In 2016, Cirque du Soleil introduced its first Broadway theatrical production at the Lyric Theatre on 42nd street in New York City. "Paramour" stars Ruby Lewis in the female lead role and is a true musical with ten original songs. The show is a Hollywood love story laced with incredible athletic circus acts. Paramour got off to a strong start grossing one million dollars for the first six shows.

Cirque du Soleil is not limited to just its famous theatrical productions. Other divisions of the company produce original TV, DVD and video programs that are distributed worldwide. The Special Events Division produces shows for public, corporate and private events. There is also a merchandising division responsible for providing all sorts of novelties, and recently Cirque introduced a fashion line of women's clothing and accessories. Cirque du Soleil begun by two street performers in little Baie-Saint Paul 30 years ago is a billion-dollar business-- and Guy Laliberte is worth over three billion dollars, ranking him among the wealthiest men in the world. Laliberte always claimed his interest in show business began when his parents took him to watch Ringling Brothers, Barnum, and Bailey Circus when he was in grade school. This led him to read the biography of P.T. Barnum, and he was hooked for life. He produced several performing arts events while attending high school. Laliberte was only 25 years old, without a steady job, living the life of a street performer when he established Cirque du Soleil in 1984. The name Cirque du Soleil, "Circus of the Sun," was Laliberte's idea because he felt the sun stands for energy and youth, and his circus is all about those two words.

The touring division of Cirque du Soleil uses colorful blue and yellow striped tents.

On October 29, 2007, Guy Laliberte announced the launch of the One Drop Foundation to fight poverty around the world by giving everyone access to clean water. Cirque du Monde sponsored by the One Drop Foundation makes use of the circus arts, folklore, popular theatre, music, dance, and the visual arts, to promote education, community involvement and public awareness of water issues. The operating costs of the foundation are covered by Laliberte's contribution of $100 million. Field activities are financed by Cirque du Soleil employees and contributions from public and private donors.

In April 2015, Laliberte sold his majority stake in Cirque du Soleil to private investors, but he continues to provide strategic and creative input to the company.

Baie-Saint Paul is a special little village on the Saint Lawrence River about 50 miles north of Quebec City. The town has a population of about 7500 and is located at the gateway to the scenic Charlevoix Valley. The village is filled with quaint historic houses and has over 30 art galleries and a wonderful, small public art museum. I have personally visited there many times and it is, indeed, a remarkable and charming French-Canadian village.

Cirque du Soleil also engages in several Canadian public service projects involving the arts. One of these is the National Circus School (Ecole National de Cirque.) The National Circus School is a professional circus school located in Montreal, Canada. Established in 1981, the premier circus school in the Americas offers professional training in circus arts. Disciplines taught include dance, acting, physical training, manipulation, balancing, acrobatics, and aerials. The arts program is accompanied by academic courses required by the province of Quebec secondary school system. After obtaining their high school diploma students may pursue higher education through the Diploma of Collegial Studies in Circus Arts. This program combines specialized training in circus and theatre arts with a general college education and awards a full college diploma. Students choose a major from five disciplines: aerials, balancing, acrobatics, manipulation, and clown acts.

The performances by the Cirque du Soleil cast of acrobats are incredible.

The need to train versatile and highly skilled artists has grown tremendously during the past 20 years as the contemporary circus arts experience, Cirque du Soleil, has grown exponentially throughout the world. The school boasts a job placement rate for graduates of 95 percent.

In addition to the National Circus School, there are many other schools around the U.S. offering professional, and sometimes degree-level, training in various circus skills, such as acrobatics, aerial acts, object manipulation (juggling), and other specialized skills. Surprisingly, the number of these schools is growing and there are also active programs in the U.K., Netherlands, Sweden, France, and Australia.

Gamma Phi Circus at Illinois State University, Bloomington, Illinois, is the oldest collegiate circus in the United States. It began as the Gamma Phi fraternity, founded in 1929 by a gymnastics instructor at the university. Gamma Phi Circus is a performing arts fraternal organization and is not affiliated with any national social fraternity or sorority; it is a registered student organization. Membership is available by audition to all full-time Illinois State students and faculty. The circus produces a "Home Show" every April before an audience of over 16,000 fans. It also produces 20 to 30 road shows each year and performs at schools, businesses, and charities. Circus alumni have gone on to perform in a variety of venues including Shrine Circuses, Disney World, Busch Gardens and Universal Studios.

The only other collegiate four-year university with a full-fledged circus program is Florida State, Tallahassee, Florida. The "Flying High Circus" is an extra-curricular activity under Florida State's Division of Student Affairs. All members of the FSU Circus are required to be degree-seeking students at Florida State University. The FSU Circus is primarily a three-ring aerial and stage presentation with no animal acts. Student performers learn about the circus including how to rig their own equipment, produce light and sound for performances, and even pitch-in to set up the circus's large tent.

The Flying High Circus was founded in 1947 as an effort to integrate women at the newly co-ed institution (Florida State had been an all-female school and officials were looking for activities to bring the young men and women together). Over the past 70 years, the circus has had wide exposure on TV and has performed all over the U.S., Canada and Europe. In addition to a travelling road show, the circus performs every spring weekend in its own tent located on the campus.

The following is a partial list of professional circus schools scattered around the U.S.:

New England Center for Circus Arts in Brattleboro, VT, Westchester Circus Arts Center in Tarrytown, NY., The Circus Center in San Francisco, CA., Philadelphia School of Circus Arts in Philadelphia, PA., The Actors Gymnasium in Evanston, IL., Sky Candy in Austin, TX., Aloft Loft Circus School in Chicago, IL.

In addition to these college and professional schools, many high schools in the U.S. offer training in circus arts; one of the most famous schools described earlier is the Sailor School in Sarasota, Florida.

Another valuable asset group helping to keep the circus tradition alive is the many museums around the Country devoted to the circus. Most of these museums are staffed by volunteers who have a love of the circus. Many of these museums offer more than just a display of circus memorabilia. The museums sponsor tours and lectures, and in some cases schedule live performances.

Ringling Brothers "Greatest Show On Earth" currently uses two separate circuses, a red and a blue, to tour the U.S.A. The routes are alternated annually to bring a new show to town each year.

TODAY

The circus has certainly had to change since Ringling Brothers ended its season early on July 16, 1956, and returned to Sarasota winter quarters. "Big Top Bows out Forever" was the headline in Life Magazine, and the New York Times headline read "The Big Top Folds Its Tents for the Last Time." The Pittsburgh paper had a cartoon showing Uncle Sam with hat in hand, tears streaming down his face, standing before a gravestone inscribed, "Here lies Ringling Brothers and Barnum and Bailey".

The birth of television almost put the American circus out of business. Thanks to the enterprising Feld brothers, the circus changed to meet the competition. It abandoned the "Big Top" and switched to the relatively new venue, the air conditioned indoor arena.

As I prepare to conclude this story about the wonderful world of the circus, Ringling Bros. and Barnum & Bailey circus has announced that after 146 years of performances, it is folding its big tent forever. The final show will be in May 2017.

Ringling Bros. two touring circuses have attracted over 10 million people each year, but a combination of problems has made the shows unprofitable. Transporting the big shows by rail and other special quirks; such as providing a traveling school for children and legal costs associated with animal activist demands have created a cost structure where an affordable ticket price is no longer a viable option.

The final blow came last year when elephants were dropped from the shows and ticket sales began to drop drastically. The elephants, the longtime mainstay of the circus, were retired because there are too many other opportunities to see animals perform on television or in Disney movies and increasing pressure from animal rights groups to ban all animal performances.

"The freak show" or sideshow is long gone, thank goodness, along with the parade and the menagerie, but the clown remains an important part of the contemporary circus along with unbelievably talented acrobats, cyclists, aerialists, and gymnasts.

Once again, as it did 50 years ago, the circus must adapt and move forward. The Cirque du Soleil model appears to be today's answer to the challenge. With no animals, continuous music, absolutely thrilling human performances in a theatrical setting, the shows are thriving. There are currently about 20 separate shows, both resident and touring, and they set an attendance record every year through good or bad times.

While Cirque du Soleil will lead the change in the circus, many smaller tent shows representing the typical circus will continue to travel the U.S.A. each year. The circus in some form will continue to be an attraction for "children of all ages" and it will endure as "The Greatest Show on Earth."

Ringling Bros. and Barnum & Bailey, 1947 Route

Ringling Bros. and Barnum & Bailey Combined Shows, Inc.,
proprietor - From Ringling Bros. and Barnum & Bailey Circus 1954 Route
Book. Provided by John Polacek.

April/May

Apr. 9 - May 11 New York City,
Madison Square Garden
May 13-21 Boston, Mass.
May 23-31 Philadelphia, Pa.

June

2-7 Washington, D. C.
9-14 Baltimore, Md.
16-21 Pittsburgh, Pa.
23 York, Pa.
24 Wilmington, Del.
25 Trenton, N. J.
26 New Brunswick, N. J.
27 Allentown, Pa.
28 Easton, Pa.
30 Albany, N. Y.

July

1 Schenectady, N. Y.
2 Utica, N. Y.
3 Syracuse, N. Y.
4 Binghamton, N. Y.

September

1-3 Denver, Col.
4 Colorado Springs, Col.
5 Pueblo, Col.
6 Trinidad, Col.
8 Amarillo, Tex.
9 Plainview, Tex.
10 Lubbock Tex.
11 Sweetwater, Tex.
12 San Angelo, Tex.
13 Abilene, Tex.
15-16 Dallas, Tex.
17 Gainesville, Tex.
18 Wichita Falls, Tex.
19 Sherman, Tex.
20 Paris, Tex.
22-23 Shreveport, La.
24 Longview, Tex.
25 Tyler, Tex.
26 Corsicana, Tex.
27-28 Fort Worth, Tex.
29 Waco, Tex.
30 Austin, Tex.

5 Elmira, N. Y.
7 Rochester, N. Y.
8 Tonawanda, N. Y.
9 Olean, N. Y.
10 Jamestown, N. Y.
11 Erie, Pa.
12-13 Cleveland, O.
14-15 Akron, O.
16 Canton, O.
17 Mansfield, O.
18 Marion, O.
19-20 Columbus, O.
21 Dayton, O.
22 Lima, O.
23-24 Toledo, O.
25-30 Detroit, Mich.
31 Jackson, Mich.

August

2-10 Chicago, Ill.
11-12 Milwaukee, Wis.
13 Madison, Wis.
14 Freeport, Ill.
15 Rockford, Ill.
16 Joliet, Ill.
18 Peoria, Ill.
19 Bloomington, Ill.
20 Champaign, Ill.
21 Danville, Ill.
22 Decatur, Ill.
23 Springfield, Ill.
25-26 Kansas City, Mo.

October

1-2 San Antonio, Tex.
3 Victoria, Tex.
4-6 Houston, Tex.
7 Lake Charles, La.
8 Alexandria, La.
9 Baton Rouge, La.
10-12 New Orleans, La.
13 Hattiesburg, Miss.
14 Jackson, Miss.
15 Greenwood, Miss.
16 Clarksdale, Miss.
17-18 Memphis, Tenn.
20-21 Nashville, Tenn.
22 Decatur, Ala.
23-24 Birmingbam, Ala.
25 Montgomery, Ala.
27-28 Atlanta, Ga.
29 Chattanooga, Tenn.
30 Knoxville, Tenn.
31 Asheville, N. C.

November

1 Spartanburg, S.C.
3-4 Richmond, Va.
5-6 Norfolk, Va.
7 Wilson, N. C.
8 Raleigh, N. C.
10 Winston-Salem, N. C
11 Charlotte, N. C.
12 Columbia, S. C.

27 Manhattan, Kan.
28 Hutchinson, Kan.
29 Great Bend, Kan.
30 Dodge City, Kan.

13 Savannah, Ga.
14-15 Jacksonville, Fla.
17-19 Miami, Fla.
21 St. Petersburg, Fla.
22 Tampa, Fla.
23 Sarasota, Fla.
End of season

BIBLIOGRAPHY

Apps, Jerry. TENTS, TIGERS AND THE RINGLING BROTHERS. Wisconsin Historical Society Press, 2007

Ballentine, Bill. WILD TIGERS AND TAME FLEAS. Literacy Licensing LLC, 2013

Bradna, Fred. THE BIG TOP. Simon and Schuster, 1952

Clausen, Connie. I LOVE YOU HONEY BUT THE SEASON'S OVER. Holt, Rinehart and Winston, 1961

Chindahl, George L. THE HISTORY OF THE CIRCUS IN AMERICA. The Claxton Printers Ltd. 1959

Culhane, John. THE AMERICAN CIRCUS. Henry Holt and Company, 1990

Daniel, Noel, editor. THE CIRCUS 1870's-1950's. Published Taschen Books, 2008

Davis, Janet M. THE CIRCUS AGE. University of North Carolina Press, 2002

Feiler, Bruce. UNDER THE BIG TOP. Harper Perennial, 2003

Fleming, Candace. THE GREAT AND ONLY BARNUM. Swartz and Wade, 2009

Hammerstrom, David. BIG TOP BOSS. University of Illinois Press, 1994

Howard, Lyn. THE SPARK CIRQUE du SOLEIL. Doubleday Division of Random House, 2006

Knaebel, Nathaniel. STEP RIGHT UP. Carroll and Graf Publishers, 2004

Loxton, Howard. THE GOLDEN AGE OF THE CIRCUS. Smithmark Publishing, 1997

May, Earl. THE CIRCUS FROM ROME TO RINGLING. Kessinger Publishing LLC, 2007

Nickel, Joe. SECRETS OF THE SIDESHOWS. University Press of Kentucky, 2005

North, Henry Ringling. CIRCUS KINGS. University Press of Florida, 2008

River, Charles. Editors. THE GREATEST SHOW ON EARTH. 2014

Saxon, A.H. P.T. BARNUM. Columbia University Press, 1983

Smyth, Betty Patterson. A FIRST OF MAY. WRB Publishing, 2012

Sutton, Felix. THE BIG SHOW A HISTORY OF THE CIRCUS. Doubleday Publishing, 1971

Walk, Debra. THE CIRCUS IN MINIATURE. The John and Mable Ringling Museum of Art Serbin Printing and Publishing, 2003

Thank You for Reading Circus.

Please help the author by posting a review on amazon.

Check out other fine books by Terry W. Lyons

Available on Amazon and at all Bookstores

DRINKING

AROUND THE

WORLD

TERRY W. LYONS

BAR HOPPING THRU AMERICA

Taverns, Bars, Saloons and Night Clubs-
AN AMERICAN HISTORY

TERRY W. LYONS

www.ingramcontent.com/pod-product-compliance
Lightning Source LLC
Chambersburg PA
CBHW060841280326
41934CB00007B/873